W9-DJE-253

REAL WORLD CUSTOMER SERVICE

Bernice B. Johnston

WARNER MEMORIAL LIBRARY
EASTERN COLLEGE
ST. DAVIDS, PA. 19087

Small Business Sourcebooks
from **Sourcebooks** Inc.
Naperville, Illinois

9-2-96

Copyright © 1996 by Bernice B. Johnston
Cover design © 1996 by Sourcebooks, Inc.

All rights reserved. No part of this book may be reproduced in any form or by any electronic or mechanical means including information storage and retrieval systems—except in the case of brief quotations embodied in critical articles or reviews, or in the case of the exercises in this book solely for the personal use of the purchaser—without permission in writing from its publisher, Sourcebooks, Inc.

Published by: **Sourcebooks, Inc.**
P.O. Box 372, Naperville, Illinois, 60566
(708) 961-3900
FAX: 708-961-2168

Editorial: Todd Stocke
Cover Design: Wayne Johnson/Dominique Raccah
Interior Design and Production: Andrew Sardina, Sourcebooks, Inc.

HF 5415.5 .J64 1996
Johnston, Bernice B., 1937-
Real-world customer service

This publication is designed to provide accurate and authoritative information in regard to the subject matter covered. It is sold with the understanding that the publisher is not engaged in rendering legal, accounting, or other professional service. If legal advice or other expert assistance is required, the services of a competent professional person should be sought.
From a Declaration of Principles Jointly Adopted by a Committee of the American Bar Association and a Committee of Publishers and Associations

The **Small Business Sourcebooks** series is designed to help you teach yourself the business essentials you need to be successful. All books in the series are available for bulk sales. Call us for information or a catalog. Other books in the series include:

- *Mancuso's Small Business Resource Guide*
- *The Internet Business Primer*
- *Your First Business Plan*
- *The Small Business Start-Up Guide*
- *Great Idea! Now What?*
- *The Small Business Legal Guide*
- *Smart Hiring*
- *How to Get a Loan or Line of Credit*

Library of Congress Cataloging-in-Publication Data
Johnston, Bernice B.,
    Real-world customer service / Bernice B. Johnston
        p.   cm. — (Small business sourcebooks)
    ISBN 1-57071-063-5 : $17.95 (hc.) — ISBN 1-57071-062-7 : $9.95 (pbk.)
    1. Customer services — Management. 2. Consumer complaints —
Management. I. Title. II. Series.
HF5415.5.J64   1995
658.8'12 — dc20
    95-36909
    CIP

Printed and bound in the United States of America.

Hardcover — 10 9 8 7 6 5 4 3 2 1
Paperback — 10 9 8 7 6 5 4 3 2 1

Acknowledgments

While I accept responsibility for all that is written here, I am not alone in its writing. Beside me stand my early colleagues who shared with me the pain of the troubled families we served; the CEOs who care about their employees and their customers and hire me to help; the workshop participants who asked for ideas; my family (Gib and Mark and Lilly and Mike and Mom and the judge and the professor) who always waited for me and make me possible; John Covey who urged me in 1991 "to lift others to higher ground—to teach the highest best within you"; Art Chenowith who critiqued the first drafts, Dean Owen who pushed me through the initial inquiry stages, Lynda Falkenstein who helped me turn the corner, and all those who said, "When are you going to finish your book? I need it!" And behind me, most of all, stands Murray McBride without whom...

Table of Contents

What Would You Say?

A Self-Assessment

Match your customer complaint skill against the experts—the customer with a complaint. Read the statements below and the possible, though perhaps extreme, range of responses that follow. On page xi, rank the order of each of the responses.

Give 1 to the best response, 2 to second best, etc., with 5 to the response you find the least satisfactory.

1. *Customer: I ordered that part months ago and I still haven't received it!*

   A. What is your name?
   B. That's terrible! It sounds like you've been really inconvenienced.
   C. Why didn't you let us know sooner that you hadn't received it?
   D. It takes six to eight weeks to fill some requests.
   E. Who knows what happens when the orders leave here!

2. *Customer: They said at the other store they could do it. If you can't help me, I'll go to your boss!*

   A. What did they say?
   B. If I didn't think someone could help, I'd want to talk with a supervisor, too.
   C. If you'd calm down, I could help you better.
   D. I understand your situation, but I have to follow the procedures.
   E. Well, you just do that!

3. *Client: Why didn't you call me back with an answer? I really don't understand why it's been over three weeks now, when you said it would be ten days.*

   A. Who did you talk to?
   B. I'd be wondering too if it had taken so long to get an answer.
   C. Please be patient. It takes time.
   D. The computer broke down.
   E. It wasn't me. I didn't work here then.

4. *Customer: I want my money back, and don't ask me for the receipt because I don't have it. I ordered this as a gift for my boss. I really looked like a %*!% fool when it didn't work.*

   A. When did you buy it?
   B. If that had happened to me, I'd have been upset too.
   C. I can help you, but there's no need to swear.
   D. It's clearly spelled out that you have to have your receipt.
   E. It's not my fault they make you have a receipt. You better to talk to my supervisor.

What Would You Say? A Self-Assessment

Rank Order   Rationale

1. _____   _____

   _____   _____

   _____   _____

   _____   _____

   _____   _____

2. _____   _____

   _____   _____

   _____   _____

   _____   _____

   _____   _____

3. _____   _____

   _____   _____

   _____   _____

   _____   _____

4. _____   _____

   _____   _____

   _____   _____

   _____   _____

   _____   _____

How did you do? While you can't predict without a doubt what a customer will say in response to any of your choices, some are more likely to get you further than others.

From least to most preferable for all customer statements:

Option E: You lose and your customer wins at great cost to everyone. While your feelings are perhaps understandable, the words sound more like those of a child than of an adult. You force your customer, who is now angrier with you than with the presenting problem, to denounce you to your supervisor. You <u>may</u> get to keep your job.

Option C: You win—if you want high marks as a dominating parent scolding a misbehaving child. When you treat someone like a child, how do you think they will behave? Like a child, of course, more often than not. If you believe your customers do not deserve help unless they behave according to your personal criteria, you are probably in the wrong job. Again, you compel your customer to complain to your supervisor. It won't be too long before your supervisor decides that if she has to field customer complaints, she doesn't need you.

Option D: The winner is the bureaucracy! What the customer hears are excuses that mean you're not going to help him. What the customer knows is that neither you nor your company care, and that rules are more important than relationships.

Option A: This can be a deceptive choice. Maybe you are one who wants to get right to the point and you figure your customers do too. You must choose your questions carefully, however. If you have the information on file, if you could solve the problem without that answer, if the customer's answer could be wrong, then you are wasting time not getting to the point.

Option B: You get a gold star! With this option everybody wins, especially your customer. You have discovered the key for working effectively with distraught complainants: refusing to let their emotions—disgust, threats, frustration, fury—get in your way of solving the problem. Some of the most solid customer relationships are built on a savvy employee's acceptance of a customer's negative feelings. A word of caution: your tone of voice must convey empathy ("I know what it's like because I have experienced something similar myself") and not a patronizing attitude.

Preface

Have you ever been the recipient of, the sender of, or the object of a letter like the following?

Dear Ms. Supervisor:

Today I had the unfortunate experience of talking with your employee Clara Clerk about my invoice, which was billed to the wrong insurance company. Upon telling Ms. Clerk about the error, she said your health clinic could not complete the paperwork as it had done for the first insurance company because it was not a major insurance contractor. "Our clinic is just too small to provide that service for every little insurance company that comes along. You'll just have to do it yourself," she said.

When I asked her to check further, she again restated her position. And then she said, "I can understand your frustration. Unfortunately, these are the rules and I don't make the rules." My response: "I know you don't make the rules; however, I have no one to talk with but you. I don't know who the rule-maker is. If you can't help me, I'd like to speak to the rule-maker."

Ms. Supervisor, I believe your Ms. Clerk has had training in some of the right words to say, but her attitude certainly does not reflect the spirit that surely was intended by the training nor any apparent empathy for the patient. In my experience, referring to the rules generally only waves a red flag in front of the customer. What the customer really hears is, "Ms. Customer, I have no intention of helping you."

When I insisted, rather heatedly at that point, on speaking with the rule-maker, she put me on hold for several minutes and returned to tell me that indeed she could bill the insurance company. "There was a change three months ago and nobody told me," she said.

Had I not been angry and demanded to push this matter further in the first place, it was very clear she would have done nothing, other than to hide behind her rule book.

She then asked me for my insurance billing information. I asked why she couldn't look it up in my patient file. She said, "It might take me days to get information. If you would just cooperate with me, I'll take care of it."

Ms. Supervisor, i suppose you can imagine, given what had already transpired, I did not appreciate being called "uncooperative," which of course I told her.

However, since she apparently is, by her own admission, slow and uninformed, I decided I should not trust this huge task to her and dug out the billing information. I do believe at this time I also told her that maybe I would apply for part of her pay since I was doing her work.

As we were finishing this transaction, I asked her name so I could note it for my records. She refused to give me her last name, saying, "I'm the only Clara here. I don't give out my last name." [Is this *her* rule again or yours?] I can appreciate people not wanting to give out their names. But if it is a policy to protect your employees' identities from customers they incense, give them an alias to use; it doesn't make sense to persist in alienating an already upset customer!

I continued to press until she finally told me. "And you can just write a letter about me if you want!" she dared. Until that moment, I had no intention of doing so. Generally I believe if an employee is that uninformed (nearly three months behind in her information), that poorly equipped to handle billing problems (the most thankless job on earth, whatever the pay), and totally unable to prevent the escalation of a simple billing error into a major confrontation, it's not the employee's fault. However, I decided to take her up on her challenge and so here is my letter.

Perhaps you can use this as an opportunity to examine how situations like these can be better managed, how to help an employee know when it's gone too far, and no matter what she does, it's going to get worse. And if she is right, that you are too small and slow to handle what seems like a simple matter to me, perhaps I should consider another health care provider. Given the enormous changes descending on the health care industry, perhaps it would be well that you inform my employer and my insurance company that you are unable to handle their business.

Sincerely,

Ms. Angry Customer

By the way, I called the clinic receptionist who was far more cooperative. "I'll be happy to give you Clara's last name," she said.

Why this book? The book you hold is a unique guide, written specifically to help employees assist customers who complain, and to avoid transforming a minor error into a major confrontation. Many books about customer service have been written for managers and supervisors in general, with only short chapters about complaint handling. While a company's dedication to excellent customer service is paramount if a company is to survive, an employee's ability to manage the inevitable complaints is the real test of excellence. And if you ask employees who spend time with the public what they want to know more about, without a doubt their first concern is how to be more effective in handling disgruntled and irate customers.

This book began many years ago, not in words on paper but in actions practiced. It also represents a special and valued partnership between me and several thousand people who collaborated with me to create the word-for-word dialogues found in the Exposure Recovery Scripts beginning on page 51.

The early years: I began my professional career on the sometimes literal firing line of complaint management when I was hired to investigate child abuse complaints in a small, isolated community in rural Oregon. During those demanding years, I adapted, as did all my co-workers, my formal training to the unique requirements of each situation. From this I developed a framework that guided my professional work with others when I left the public sector for a private practice of management consulting and training. Over the years, as I worked with different types of complaint management systems in many different organizations, I modified the components and tested, fine-tuned, and retested. You will read the results of those efforts in the first part of the book. These elements I still present in seminars and help my clients install in the workplace.

The partnership: In 1986 I began conducting open-to-the-public customer relations training programs nationwide, which several thousand people attended. As part of the workshops, participants described their real-life problems with customers by jotting down their questions and handing them in for my suggestions. In the second half of the book, I use those problems and those questions, which are the same questions asked in seminars today, along with suggested responses. What you will read are scripted dialogues just as you would hear should you attend one of my workshops.

Is this book for you? Yes—if you're on the firing line and the complaining customer looks to you for help. Yes—if you train those who handle customer complaints. Yes—if you have little time, money, or inclination to train complaint handlers. Yes—if you want others to become more knowledgeable about complaint management in all its aspects. Yes—if you want an easy-to-use guide and reference book.

How to use the book. First, familiarize yourself with the Table of Contents. *Survival Strategies* deals with systems and processes that establish a framework for guiding your actions. *Exposure Protection* contains suggestions for building credibility. *Exposure Reduction* presents "rules" to protect yourself from making situations worse. Here you can also find out what part the mind plays. *Exposure Avoidance* holds ideas you can give your boss for preventing problems and identifying hot spots in advance. *Exposure Recovery* lays out the process to use once a complaint surfaces and offers Sentence Maps to provide you with useful phrases to learn. The heart of the book lies in the *Exposure Recovery Scripts*—word-for-word dialogue to use when you need to talk with a complaining customer, the rationale for the wording, and tips. You might find it helpful to glance through this section first to get an understanding of its layout.

Throughout the book you will find charts, checklists, and case examples of complaint handling—bad ("Sink...") and good ("...or Swim"). At the end of each section, you can complete a Plan of Action to help you implement significant ideas.

After using the ideas in this book for a short time, you may feel it's not nearly so difficult as it once was to handle your share of the millions of complaints made annually. You may even come to relish the challenge and take pride in the results. Or as one of my workshop participants said, "I really like working with people who complain. I love to see them come in smokin' and go out smilin'!"

Introduction

Nobody Knows You're Swimming Naked Until The Tide Goes Out

You swim slowly out into the warm water. The snorkel mask fits tight around your eyes. You swim a little deeper, testing the snorkel and the air balance. Perfect! Relaxed now, you glance around. The brightly colored fish look at you. They move on.

Swimming back to the top, you pop above the surface, blow the water through the snorkel, and look around. The sun sparkles on the blue sea. You wave at the people on the beach and they wave back. You dive again, finding the water not so deep this time. You touch a shell. You brush away some seaweed. You stare at a tiny, bright yellow-tailed fish, and again you surface. You wave at the people. They wave back. And down you go again. This time, you're in even more shallow water. Your snorkel clears the top of the water, and you swim-crawl on the sandy bottom, feeling the gritty particles against your palms, the sun on your back.

Suddenly the surf recedes. The sand that a moment ago felt almost soft as you rubbed it between your fingers now feels rough and scrabbly and scratchy against your belly. Where a moment ago you were floating gently on top of the waves, you are now grounded as the tide goes out. You spit saltwater through your snorkel, pull off the mask, rub the water from your eyes, look up at the beach to wave. Where a moment before there had been friendly faces and friendly waves, there are now folks pointing and laughing. You look around to see what they're pointing and laughing at, and suddenly discover it's you. You look down.

You're naked, exposed, no longer the svelte swimmer everybody envied. Too much fat here, not enough there; too much hair there, not enough here. The people on the beach laugh a moment longer. Then they turn to look at another swimmer emerging from the water—a beautiful body, a handsome figure, well-proportioned, looking great in the latest high fashion suit.

Most of us share that "worst nightmare"—one we hope will never come true—running down the street, swimming in the water, dancing in the ballroom, and suddenly discovering you're naked. You don't know where to turn. There's nothing to cover you. You're exposed.

Companies are very much like this. They look good. They have great products, great service, quality, and excellence—until the day a complaint surfaces. How you handle that complaint compared to how you handled the complaint before, compared to how your competitors handle complaints, compared to the customer's expectations, determines whether you come out of it looking great, beautiful, and confident. Or you emerge ugly, misshapen, embarrassed—exposed.

This book specifically addresses the topic of managing customer complaints. You'll find diagrams, processes, and most importantly, scripts—*exactly what to say*. Customers and employees alike make mistakes in spite of our best efforts. The tough customers, the critics, and the complainers give us opportunities to do better—to change, to smooth the way. They give us a second chance to make things easier for those who often can't make sense out of our best efforts.

It's said that if customers like what you do, they'll tell two or three other people. If they don't like what you do, they'll tell 12 to 15 others. And 13% of those who don't like what you do will tell 20 or more. It's a scary thought, isn't it, that right this moment, there may be 13% of your unhappy customers telling 20 others about you?

You may not have the research to determine exactly what an unhappy customer costs your own organization, but here's a formula you can apply: If your company loses one customer a day, and that customer spends $5.00 per week, it will cost your organization $94,900 in annual lost revenue (365 customers times $5 times 52 weeks = $94,900). Translate that to your business: when your customer walks in the door or calls you on the phone, what amount of revenue does that customer represent? What would it cost you if you lost only one customer a day? Would it cost you your raise? Could it cost you your job?

From Customer to Competitor

Once upon a time there was a man by the name of Rupert Sanders (not his real name). He was not a pleasant man. He was crotchety and opinionated. He had no sense of humor. His co-workers (I was one) ignored him.

Rupert Sanders owned a small farm that required electricity to run the irrigation pumps. One summer Mr. Sanders got into a dispute with the local power company about his bill. He tried to work out the disagreements, but neither the employees nor the manager heeded his complaints. As a captive customer, Mr. Sanders couldn't unplug and take his business elsewhere, there was no natural gas to convert to, and only electricity could run the pumps.

Because he was not smart, because he was not rich, because he did not know anybody important, because he had no humor, and because he was disagreeable, the utility discounted him. It did not listen. What began as small and resolvable escalated as Mr. Sanders wrote letters to the newspaper and filed official complaints. The utility still did not notice, but the tide had started to recede.

Perhaps the utility had expected him to give up as many of us would have, but Mr. Sanders was not one to live with indifferent treatment. He decided to form his own electric company. To buck an established monopoly is a formidable task at best, but he persisted and brought together others (maybe the 20 others in the community who were also unhappy with the utility?). It took ten years, but Mr. Sanders did indeed succeed. Eventually his utility forced from the community the very monopoly that had mistreated him and been so inattentive to his complaint.

Of course, the monopoly fought it, but when the tide went out, the utility was naked and not a pleasant sight to see. The irrigation pump dispute cost the utility $10,000,000 and 50,000 customers. Today, Mr. Sanders' utility has those 50,000 customers and it continues to make life uncomfortable for the monopoly, like sand fleas biting, stinging, and annoying.

You may not have a Rupert Sanders haunting your operation, a Rupert Sanders created by your inattention to a complaint. But ask yourself as you review your customer transactions, do your customers feel better as a result of the time they spend with you or do they feel worse? Clearly, you personally can do little about some organizational problems other than speak to your boss about them in a professional manner when opportunities arise. However, within your circle of influence, within your time with a customer, you can provide a bridge, a helping hand. You can listen, you can explore, you can find alternatives. You can stay afloat.

What Is Complaint Management?

Complaint management is not about making the customer happy.

Happiness is not *having* a complaint at all—ever. Happiness is exceeding the customer's expectations. But once expectations are not met, once there is a problem, once there is a concern, once the customer has to return an item because something went haywire (whether you went haywire or the customer went haywire), happiness becomes an elusive goal.

Once there is a complaint, your goal is **to help the customer be successful with the options now available.**

Examine your own experience as a customer. Take the common hotel reservation, for instance. When you arrive at a hotel, happiness is your room ready and available. If it is not, the clerk may suggest that you wait in the restaurant, perhaps even offer to buy you a drink and dinner, while they prepare your room. Are you happy? Likely not. You may get drunk, you may get fed well. But while you eat and drink, you're anxious about your room and your changed plans. You're upset. Eventually, you **will** get your room; you **will** be successful. Happy? Probably not. As a matter of fact, every time thereafter when you make reservations in that hotel (and because they handled the problem appropriately, you will), you'll remind the clerk who takes the reservation, no matter how many years later, of the one time your room was not ready and you were inconvenienced.

Complaints always live longer than the time you spend fixing them. They are the most important transactions you will engage in.

Chapter One

Survival Strategies

✓ *Checklist*
Survival Strategies

❏ *Use a complaint management system*

❏ *Use a systematic complaint management process*

❏ *Listen to learn*

❏ *Understand emotional escalation*

❏ *Take care of yourself*

Complaints don't have to escalate out of control, resulting in lost customers and disastrous public relations. By carefully applying the survival strategies described below, you can contain potentially damaging situations, and in many cases, strengthen your valuable relationships with customers.

Use a Complaint Management System

For an effective, yet simple-to-use complaint management system, you need:

✓ *Checklist*
Complaint Management System

❏ *Your goal*

❏ *The guiding principle*

❏ *A systematic problem-solving process*

❏ *The method*

- **Your goal**: To help the customer be successful with the options now available.

- The **guiding principles*** of:
  - Rebuilding relationships
  - Establishing communication
  - Creating trust
  - Developing mutual understanding
  - Resolving problems

---

*To be a principle an item must apply all the time. The idea is simply (1) to do what is consistent with the principles and (2) to avoid doing anything that would violate any of them.

- **A systematic problem-solving process:** See *Figure 1* depicting the three-stage *Complaint Management Model* on the following page.

- **The method:** A two-way communication process between you and the people who depend on you for help. See the *Exposure Recovery* section beginning on page 37.

 **SINK**

Because my work takes me traveling across the country, I have many opportunities to observe and suffer from bad examples of hotel service. Most hotels can do well if you stay only one night, but it takes special effort to provide service that is consistently good over several days.

On one three-night stay in one of the West Coast's more expensive chain hotels, for example, I experienced the following:

Night One: Okay, other than they didn't have any record of my reservation, although I had a confirmation notice.

Night Two: At 2 A.M., a man using his key and carrying his suitcase entered my room. He was even more startled than I to discover the hotel clerk had rented my room to him, too!

Day Two: Room service forgot to include silverware for my breakfast tray. The swimming pool, scheduled to be unlocked at 9 A.M., was still locked at noon, no explanation. The room's linens had not been restocked by the end of the day.

Night Three: I did not receive my wake-up call for 7 A.M. I did receive someone's 4 A.M. call.

Day Three: Room service forgot to include silverware for my breakfast tray, milk for the berries, and butter for the toast. I discovered a broken dish under the bed. The washcloth had a hole the size of a small saucer ripped from its center.

Several days after I wrote a letter of complaint to the president of the hotel chain, his assistant called me to apologize for him. She concluded by saying, "I have seen the president upset before but I've never seen him as mad as he was when he finished reading about what happened to you. He was so mad he almost wet his pants!"

Do you think the president would be happy to know how his assistant described him? Tact is a useful quality to develop.

Use a Systematic Complaint Management Process

If you are to succeed in resolving customer complaints, the best approach is a systematic step-by-step process, such as the one depicted in *The Complaint Management Model* (Figure 1).

When you do not use a systematic process, you'll find it difficult to pinpoint where breakdowns occur. More importantly, when you are successful, you'll find it difficult to repeat what you did that made the transaction go well.

FIGURE 1. THE COMPLAINT MANAGEMENT MODEL

PROBLEM RESOLUTION			
STAGES OF INQUIRY	**I-DISCOVERY**	**II-CONFIRMATION**	**III-RESOLUTION**
Customer Behavior	Inquiry Request Question Complaint	Acknowledgment	Acceptance
Employee Objectives	1. Establish relationship 2. Suspend own values 3. Further inquiry 4. Maintain composure	1. Isolate critical issue(s) (situation, problem, transaction) 2. Represent business	1. Develop plan of action 2. Gain commitment
Employee Responsibility	1. Attend 2. Listen 3. Respond	1. Attend, listen, respond 2. Identify 3. Clarify	1. Attend, listen, respond 2. Select strategy 3. Negotiate agreement/ action
Primary Skill	Empathic listening	1. Appraisal 2. Problem-solving	1. Negotiation 2. Decision-making
Outcome	1. Relationship established 2. Interchangeable exchange	1. Critical issue(s) identified 2. Solution(s) generated	1. Issue resolved 2. Follow-up

Although the process pictured in the model may seem time-consuming, it often can be completed in less than ten minutes. Of course, the more complex the issue, the longer it may take to resolve.

SWIM

Sometimes customers are so understanding of a mistake you make, there seems to be little need to compensate them when an error does occur. However, if you can make an adjustment, you may make a friend for life.

Two anxieties permeate every flyer's not-so-sub-conscious: "Will my luggage make it?" and "Will my room be ready?" For the frequent traveler, the room reservation system worldwide seems stalled in the dark ages. Even the confirmed room, deposit guaranteed, is no guarantee. Here's how one hotel made reparation.

"Yes, I know we gave you a 50% discount on your guest room already because of your association membership," acknowledged the clerk, when a patron questioned her reduced bill. "And, yes, you did say you weren't bothered by the mix-up here at the front desk last night. But there was no excuse as far as we're concerned so there'll be no charge for your room at all."

When you own up to the mistake and you have a true customer commitment, you can reverse an unpleasant experience with a pleasant surprise.

As you work through the complaint management process, each stage—*Discovery, Confirmation,* and *Resolution*—should be completed before you proceed to the next. Unless you are confident you have a relationship with your customer and the customer acknowledges you understand her complaint **from her point of view** (Stage One), it is premature and unproductive to move into Stage Two.

A common problem for the seasoned professional is moving too fast, jumping from the initial complaint to an unsatisfactory plan of action. For example:

Customer: My electric bill's wrong. It's $2,000.

Employee: We've received many complaints lately about high bills because we just installed a new computer program. I'll tell our trouble shooter to add your account to the list.

Customer: You don't understand. The bill is too low. Usually it runs $3,000 a month. I sure don't want to get hit with the difference later in the year!

This employee acted on a preconceived idea, an assumption based on superficial discovery.

SINK

Have you ever felt like you were invisible, that you really don't exit? Maybe this experience is one you have lived through, too.

When I arrived at the doctor's office, I let the receptionist know I was there to keep my appointment. I sat near her desk reading a tattered *Reader's Digest*, and waited to see the doctor. Forty-five minutes past my appointment time, I asked her how much longer it would be. "Oh, I didn't see you sitting there. The doctor called. He had an emergency and won't be in today."

An observant eye will serve you well when you are responsible for managing a customer's time.

It takes considerable self-discipline to listen to complaining customers: to truly listen, to understand the world from their perspective, to see the problem and the consequences through their eyes. A systematic process will help you avoid the trap of preconceived notions about customers' needs and expectations.

Listen to Learn

If you listen effectively, you can:

- Gauge the emotional investment of the customer in the problem and the solution.

- Gain information about what's important to the customer.

- Learn new ways to continue your business with the customer despite the complaint.

Understand Emotional Escalation

What happens when the customer becomes emotionally invested in the problem? What is the thought process when expectations are not met?

- Level One—*Disappointment:* "It's broken. I'll call them."

- Level Two—*Frustration:* "They keep putting me on hold."

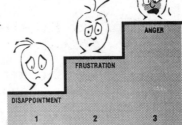

- Level Three—*Anger:* "Why do they keep transferring me from one person to another? Don't they know what's going on? Don't they talk to each other in that place? I probably should never have bought this from them to begin with."

  - *Thinking*: "I am so angry with how they're treating me, I think I'll take my business elsewhere.

  - *Feeling:* "This is ridiculous. I'm getting even angrier. Why are they treating me this way? They're making me so upset. I feel terrible about this relationship. I really feel like making them as miserable as I am!"

  - *Doing*: "They can't treat me this way! Why should I put up with this anymore? They're not paying attention to me. I'm going to do it. I'm going to move my business somewhere else, and I'm going to write a letter to the president and tell her exactly what happened!"

And now you are naked, exposed to the world, in spite of your commitment to quality and to excellence.

Please notice, although the customer was **disappointed** with the product quality, he was **mad** at the treatment he received.

There is another aspect of escalation to consider. Because we tend to mirror those around us, unless we're on guard, we get angry, sad, or hurt in turn when a distraught customer complains. That makes two of us then who are reacting with passion. The earlier in the escalation process you can intervene, indicate you understand the problem and are ready to act, the more satisfying your job will be...and the less stressful it will be for both you and the customer.

A superior complaint management system should enable you to intervene at the earliest sign of exposure. It follows then that **your organization would never let a customer's problem escalate beyond disappointment.**

Should it escalate, however, your immediate goal is to listen and to respond so that you can bring the customer's anger level down to the point where you can negotiate.

FIGURE 2. THE RELATIONSHIP BETWEEN ANGER AND REASON

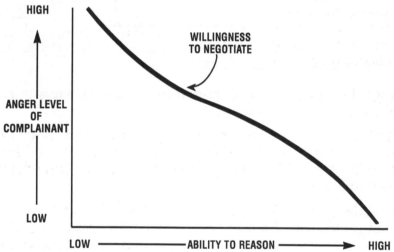

From Technical Assistance Research Programs Institute for member agencies of the Consumer Affairs Council at the request of the U.S. Office of Consumer Affairs, Sept. 30, 1985.

Take Care of Yourself

You can be the most brilliant, well-trained complaint manager ever hired by your company, **BUT** if you are not kind to yourself, it really doesn't matter how brilliant and well-trained you are. Working with people is always stimulating. Working with complaining people is challenging at its best and ruinous at its worst. You are in control of which end of the continuum best describes you.

The most common personal survival strategies probably sound suspiciously like the "advice" your mother gave you when you were little:

- Get a good night's rest (six to eight hours, at least four nights a week).

- Eat a well-balanced hot meal at least four days a week. Avoid hard-to-digest foods and heavy meals when you know the day is going to be particularly demanding. Your body will have to choose where to focus its energy—on the demanding events or on digesting your food. If it chooses the former too often, your stomach will suffer. If it chooses the latter, your customers will suffer.

- Exercise regularly. Select what works well for you. Find tension relieving activities to do at work. Walking at breaks and stretching every time you look at the clock or when someone interrupts you are good starts.

- Examine your use of cigarettes, alcohol, and other drugs to reduce or eliminate destructive habits.

- Plan for fun and humor breaks throughout the day.

Mother Nature seems to have dictated that as we grow older, things fall off, fall down, and fall out as a matter of course. An unhealthy lifestyle coupled with a demanding job can make it happen much sooner than Mother Nature planned.

You label it "stress." In fact it is **dis**tress that can cause you to react unproductively. Each of us responds differently to provocative events. But it's not the job and it's not the event; it's your unique reaction to it that makes it distressful.

Take some time to learn about distress and the damage it does over time. The more knowledgeable you are about it, the more understanding you can be of others in demanding jobs and of your customers who are highly likely to be under great stress when they have a complaint.

SWIM

Subsequent events may invalidate information you give your customer. If you can take the initiative to relay the new information, though it's not necessarily your responsibility, you will endear yourself to your boss and to your customer.

Imagine how I felt, as a customer, when the clerk phoned me with an update. "When you called here earlier this morning," she said, "I told you the Chief Engineer would be back before lunch and could call you then. I understand he's been delayed. I know you're real busy and I didn't want you to put off doing something if you were waiting for him to call you back."

I made sure not only her boss, but also the CEO heard about her thoughtfulness

It's not just seeing the world through the eyes of your customer, it's acting on that observation.

PLAN OF ACTION		
The three most important ideas I gained from this section:	I intend to use this idea when my customer/my boss/I/other:	When I applied this idea the result was:
Date 1.		Date
Date 2.		Date
Date 3.		Date

Chapter Two

Exposure Protection

Communicate: "To exchange thoughts, messages, or information."

Seems simple enough, doesn't it? Our experience tells us, however, that it isn't that easy!

✓ *Checklist*
Exposure Protection
❑ *Knowledge*
❑ *Act-as-if principal*
❑ *Keeping track of customers*

Why Do People Act the Way They Do?

Many customers' actions totally baffle us, but people do come with instructions! The problem is that we don't pay any more attention to people instructions than we do to dishwasher instructions or kite-building instructions or the instructions that came with the car.

While the obvious does not always tell us what it seems to, there are clues on how to approach or communicate with another. In the field of customer relations, data-gathering skills are critical. Each piece of information guides you toward the best way of getting your message across. Getting your message across accurately and with understanding takes time and interest in your receiver. Patience doesn't hurt either!

Remember, without exposure protection, you stand naked before your customers—and vulnerable. The more you know and the more you act like you know, the more protected you will be when your customer seeks redress.

SINK

Before customers can do business with many companies, they are required to give many details about themselves and fill out forms before they will be accepted as customers. Do you ever wonder what they do with all that information they gather, besides sell it to someone else?

When I made the special trip across town to pick up my order at the time it was promised, the printer's assistant said it would not be ready until the following day. "Why didn't you call me?" I asked. "We didn't have your number," he replied. "What's that?" I asked, pointing out my phone number where he had written it on his order form.

Do you think he was embarrassed?

Knowledge

To be a competent and effective complaint manager, you need in-depth knowledge in the seven areas listed below. On a scale of 1 (little or no working knowledge) to 5 (thorough, extensive, comprehensive expertise), how do you rate? How would your complainants rate you?

> ✓ *Checklist*
> **Knowledge**
> ❑ *Your company*
> ❑ *Your products and services*
> ❑ *Customers*
> ❑ *Salesmanship*
> ❑ *Functional knowledge*
> ❑ *Technical knowledge*
> ❑ *Business economy*

- **Your company:** Its history, its organization, its goals. *Your Score:* _____

- **Your products and services:** Their benefits, their value to the customer, their costs. *Your Score:* _____

- **Customers:** Their situation, needs, wants, perceptions, most likely fears. *Your Score:* _____

- **Salesmanship:** Your ability to influence or gain acceptance of a change, condition, or idea. *Your Score:* _____

- **Functional knowledge:** Nontechnical skills, especially communication and creativity. *Your Score:* _____

- **Technical knowledge:** Policies, procedures, resources, authority, responsibility, and accountability. *Your Score:* _____
- **Business economy:** Current conditions affecting your customer's ability to use the alternatives you provide. *Your Score:* _____

Act-As-If Principle

When you're on the phone, you must act as if the customer is sitting before you, face-to-face. The greatest barriers to effective phone communication are attention-diverters—not the customer's attention, but yours! Nearly 50% of the information about your customer's state of mind comes from the words used and the vocal qualities (pitch, tone, speed, and volume). A short daydream or a wave at a colleague across the room may distract you just enough to miss the key to your customer's success.

Keeping Track of Customers

The job of the customer relations professional includes four main functions: planning, organizing, doing, and controlling.

You PLAN your work based on your organization, direction, and understanding of your responsibilities. ORGANIZING your work means using time effectively, following appropriate company policies and procedures, developing your own schedules, to-do lists, and systems where necessary. The next step then is to get started DOING...putting your plan into action, following the process you laid out. The last step, the CONTROLLING function, frequently gets overlooked. After each call, after each completed transaction, ask yourself:

- What did I accomplish?
- Was my objective met?
- What further action should be taken?
- How did this enhance the relationship I have with the customer?

These are especially critical questions to answer when you handle customer complaints.

PLANNING
What will I do?

CONTROLLING
Did it work
like I planned?

**Customer
Success**

ORGANIZING
How will
I do it?

DOING
Putting it into action

SWIM

Busy people welcome any offering you can devise to make their personal lives more comfortable or easier. They are likely to seek you out whenever possible and stay your customer for life.

I became enamored of a limousine driver I met at Chicago's O'Hare Airport. I even relished using that airport because of how he took charge of me with great patience and understanding even when I was cranky and tired. At the end of the day, it was common to find a note from him to meet him in the hotel lounge where he waited with my favorite drink in hand—his idea after learning of my likes and dislikes as he listened to my life monologues delivered from the back seat of the limo. "It's okay, we've got plenty of time," he said. "Just sit back and relax for a minute. You deserve it."

On one memorable occasion, I was late and afraid I would miss the plane, especially since I was hand-carrying my luggage. It was only with his extraordinary help that I made it and I told him so. "Hey, I know your trips here are pretty rare," he replied, "and I'm not going to retire off the business you give me. But if it takes running interference through the airport and putting your suitcase up here in the overhead every time—see where I'm stowing it?—to make sure you make it, then that's what I'll do! See you in six months. Enjoy your flight!"

Why would your customer seek out any other service provider when you obviously care about her and demonstrate in everything you do a deep understanding and appreciation of her wishes?

PLAN OF ACTION		
The three most important ideas I gained from this section:	*I intend to use this idea when my customer/my boss/I/other:*	*When I applied this idea the result was:*
Date 1.		*Date*
Date 2.		*Date*
Date 3.		*Date*

Chapter Three

Exposure Reduction

The Rules

Follow the rules below to minimize your exposure risk:

- **Perception is the truth.**

It doesn't matter what the facts are, it is what the customer believes them to be. You can make customers see your point of view or you can see it from theirs. The latter is better and easier—start with where your customer is.

- **Fix the problem, don't fix blame.**

It does not matter who did it—you, your company, or the customer. Fix it first, then figure out what or who went wrong.

✓ *Checklist*
Rules for Exposure Reduction

- ❑ *Perception is the truth*
- ❑ *Fix the problem, don't fix blame*
- ❑ *Don't take it personally*
- ❑ *Empathize, don't sympathize*
- ❑ *Don't confess your sins*
- ❑ *Educate for future perfect*
- ❑ *Eliminate the word "why" from your vocabulary*
- ❑ *Apply the platinum rule*
- ❑ *Avoid defensiveness*
- ❑ *The customer is all you have*

SINK

Some happenings seem almost supernatural:

At 3:55 on a Friday afternoon, I called the customer service department of a mail order company to ask about the status of an order. "Please hold for the next available operator," said the computer. After I "held" for fifty minutes, the voice of the computer spoke these mystical words: "Our business hours are 9:00 A.M. to 4:45 P.M., Monday through Friday. Please call back during our business hours." Click. Dial tone.

There perhaps is no more frustrating experience for a customer than becoming trapped in a nonhuman system. When you can bring a system problem to the attention of the system keeper, and it gets fixed, your reward is small but significant: you will never have to deal with that problem again—unlike people problems, which tend not to stay fixed.

- **Don't take it personally.**

Your customer is swearing at the situation or the company, not at you. (After all, if he *really* knew you, he might have an even better name to call you!) It's your choice: once you tell him you don't like his language, *you* have chosen to personalize it. If he swore at you in Russian and you didn't understand the language, would you be offended then?

- **Empathize, don't sympathize.**

"Mr. Customer, I can understand how disappointed you must be with the delay. Let's see what I can do to speed things up."

NOT

"Mr. Customer, I honestly don't know why the salesman can't do things any faster."

- **Don't confess your sins.**

Most of us get into trouble not from talking too much, but from telling too much. Customers only need to know what you're going to do to ease their situations. They don't need to know your problems; they have enough of their own. They don't have to know your computer isn't working. (Yes, I know—it may be down. But unless you tell him, the customer doesn't even know you *have* a computer. What did you do BC—Before Computer? "Mr. Customer, it will take me a few minutes. I'll call you back within the hour with the information.")

- **Educate for future perfect.**

Don't condemn for failing at past perfect: "Why didn't you call us when it didn't work?"

BETTER

"Next time, perhaps you could give me a call before you try fixing it yourself—I may be able to give you some pointers that will make it easier. I have one of these myself."

SWIM

Sometimes customers are less conscientious than you would like them to be. They may take the easy way out and avoid doing what you think is their share. For some companies this is a problem they overcome with hefty deposits and strong warnings to ensure customer compliance. The creative enterprise studies their customer's usual behavior and turns the challenge into a customer benefit.

One such small business rents equipment to skiers. The owner did a little skier behavior research (he went searching for the skis that did not get returned) and now advertises:

"We know you're real tired after skiing all day. Don't bother bringing your skis, poles, and boots back to our rental shop. Just leave them at the hotel at the foot of the mountain and we'll pick them up."

You can be an enforcer, imposing stiffer penalties, or you can be an enabler, "turning lemons into lemonade."

SINK

To be a customer, one has to abide by the many rules and regulations that companies impose on them. Restaurants have their share of the nonsensical.

"I'd like to sit by the window," I told the restaurant hostess. "You can't sit there. We only seat parties of four by the window," she said, seating me in the back. Shortly after that, a single diner was seated at the table by the window. "Why was he seated there when you wouldn't let me?" I asked. "Oh, he's a walk-in—he didn't have a reservation and you did," she answered.

And have you ever wondered why so many restaurants give their best views to parties of four or more? Once they have glanced at the view, they never look at it again; spirited conversation takes over. Wouldn't it make more sense to give singles the view? They have no one to talk with and they are less likely to block out the view for others who are seated away from it.

Anything you can do in your organization to cut down or eliminate customer-unfriendly internal rules will reduce the number of complaints and unhappy customers you do business with.

- **Eliminate the word "why" from your vocabulary.**

It puts people on the defensive. It reminds them of "Why didn't you hang up your clothes?" "Why didn't you put gas in the car?" "Why didn't you floss?" Why questions are usually not questions, but accusations. And most people don't know "why."

- **Apply the platinum rule.**

Treat others the way *they* want to be treated. This rule differs from the Golden Rule you learned as a child: Do unto others as you would have them do unto you. The Golden Rule would be great if the world was just like you, but it's not. You have to individualize and hear each complaint as unique to that customer.

For example, when you are a customer you need bottom-line answers, and the sooner the better. Your analytical Customer Jones, however, needs to hear all the details. And your amiable Customer Smith works best when you take time for relationship building.

SWIM

It is advantageous to your business to anticipate the needs of your customers. This is easily done through a review of your records, noting the buying habits and patterns they have established over the years. Combining customer history with the future as you know it to be—upcoming holidays, seasonal adjustments, eoonomic trends, etc.—can bring business in the door and establish your value to the customer.

I know of a sole proprietor in a highly competitive, customer intensive business who makes a habit of thumbing through his client records before each holiday.

He then gets on the phone. "I was just looking through my records and see you're about due for a permanent. With the holidays coming up and that trip you're taking, would you like to come in next week so you won't have to fuss with your hair while you're on vacation?"

When your customers find you invaluable and indispensable, they will overlook occasional errors much the same as a friend who accepts your occasional misstep.

- **Avoid defensiveness.**

Hotel clerk: How was your stay?

Guest: First time my room's been the right one in all the years I've stayed here.

Clerk: You must have given us the wrong information if you've been in the wrong room.

Guest: I gave you the right information. It's just that nobody pays attention to it.

Clerk: I'm sure it would not have happened if it had been in our records.

Guest: Trust me. I've been staying here every month for longer than you are old. I know what's going on. Look it up and see for yourself.

BETTER

Hotel clerk: How was your stay?

Guest: First time my room's been the right one in all the years I've stayed here.

Clerk: I'm delighted to hear it. I'll look forward to seeing you again soon. Can I make another reservation for you—since we did so well?

- **The customer is all you have.**

Every decision you make must be based on this awareness.

The Dominant Brain

Over the last several decades, researchers have studied the behavior of people whose neural cable connecting the two major brain hemispheres has been severed. From their work in the fields of strokes and epilepsy, they found that each hemisphere tends to have a specialty. The left hemisphere controls the right side of the body and specializes in intuitive activities. Emotions seem to stem from the right hemisphere while fact-finding activities originate in the left. Individuals can be predisposed to be either left or right hemisphere dominant, although the exchange of information between the two hemispheres is so rapid, the distinction blurs.

While the brain's activities are far more complicated than can be described here, the diagram on page 30 shows a rudimentary sketch of its operations as it relates to our subject matter.

An angry customer who is left-brain dominant is inclined to be methodical and systematic, chronological in presentation, often has the documentation handy, and seems confident and self-controlled. She wants you to listen to the complete presentation to the end and agree with the logic of her needs.

> *For example:* "I wrote you a letter on March 2 and I have called you three times in the last month. I again sent you the information via certified mail and I have the signed receipt in front of me that you received my letter on April 7. Don't you think

you could have at least had the common courtesy to get back to me with an answer?"

Note the numbers, the facts, and the underlying anger.

An upset right-brain dominant customer tends to be assertive and volatile. He puts feelings over facts, does most of the talking, needs you to *do* rather than analyze, and wants you to act on the basis of his emotional assessment.

> *For example:* "I'll bet I've written or called you a hundred times to get you to do something about this mess! And don't give me any of those 'the computer's been down' or 'we've been sick' excuses either! You don't know what kind of trouble you've gotten me into! I'll probably lose my job if you don't answer my letter and tell me what's going on!"

Note the broad generalities and the obvious anger.

One of the most important aspects to remember: no matter how left-brained and logical your customer may be, once the emotions become engaged the right hemisphere "takes over" and feelings can escalate quickly.

When one becomes emotionally invested, not only is there a physiological change in the body (blood pressure raises, adrenaline flow increases, heart races), there is also a similar change in the brain: its chemistry alters as well. You will be no more successful in quieting someone's emotions by telling the individual to "calm down!" than you would be saying, "slow your heart down!" Waiting it out, letting the anger dissipate, and listening with understanding but without comment give you your best opportunity to succeed in defusing a highly charged customer.

THE DOMINANT BRAIN

Left Hemisphere

Rational/Analytic Functions:
1. Facts
2. Sequential
3. Speech
4. Math
5. Reading

Right Hemisphere

Creative/Intuitive Functions:
1. Feelings
   Afraid
   Happy
   Sad
   Angry
   Confused
2. Spatial
3. Artistic
   Painting
   Singing
   Dancing
4. Body Language
5. Swearing

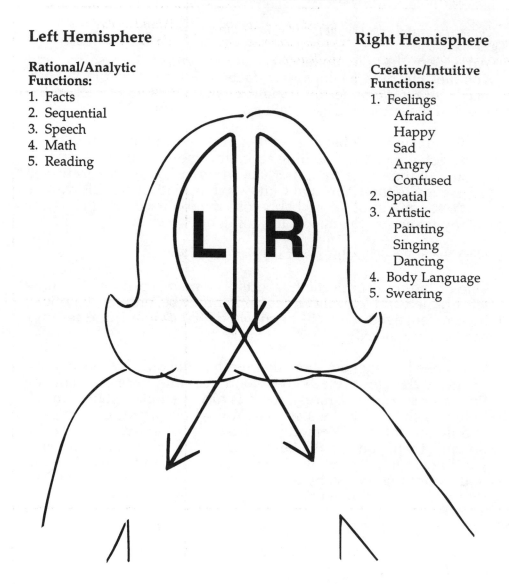

PLAN OF ACTION		
The three most important ideas I gained from this section:	*I intend to use this idea when my customer/my boss/I/other:*	*When I applied this idea the result was:*
Date 1.		Date
Date 2.		Date
Date 3.		Date

Chapter 4

Exposure Avoidance—The Tools

The suggestions listed below generally need the support and resources of your management to implement. They are useful in preventing complaints and identifying hot spots.

- **Customer surveys.**
Ask your customers formally by hiring a firm specialized in researching customer preferences.

OR

Stand outside the door of your business and ask customers informally as they leave:

- "What one thing could we have done to improve your experience with us?" and then...
- "What one other thing could we have done to improve your experience with us?"

✓ *Checklist*
**Exposure
Avoidance
—The Tools**

- ❏ *Customer surveys*
- ❏ *Employee surveys*
- ❏ *Focus groups*
- ❏ *Employee/customer problem-solving groups*
- ❏ *Training*
- ❏ *Complaint logs*
- ❏ *Ongoing complaint analysis*
- ❏ *Brainstorming for zero-defect standards*
- ❏ *Complaint case studies for universal examination*
- ❏ *Benchmarking*

SINK

How a meeting room is set up can either positively or negatively affect the outcome of a meeting or training session. Facilitators, trainers, executive assistants, and executives themselves spend many hours before an important meeting thinking through the room arrangements. Seldom, it seems, does the set-up staff attend to those carefully thought-out plans.

When I entered the meeting room, I saw it had not been set up according to the diagram and letter of instructions I had sent three weeks before. "This will all have to be rearranged," I told the set-up man. "You should have sent us some instructions," he said. "But I did," I protested. "Well, I never got them," he answered. "Just what were you told?" I asked. "Read it for yourself, lady," he answered, handing me his clipboard. I lifted the page to read the back of his detail sheet. Underneath were my diagram and letter of instructions. When I pointed it out to him, he said, "Well that's the first time I've seen that. It wasn't here before!"

What can you do to prevent a similar absurd predicament arising with one of your customers?

• **Employee surveys.**
Ask employees about their ideas, concerns, complaints, etc. This is best conducted by an external consulting firm. It too should be done on a regular schedule.

• **Focus groups.**
This is a group of customers specially selected (and usually compensated for their time) who are brought together and asked for their opinions about a number of issues of concern to the company.

• **Employee/customer problem-solving groups**.
This group is brought together to work on an issue of mutual interest, i.e., "How could we assist you in improving your market so that we can continue to be your supplier?"

• **Training**.
Invite customers to in-house workshops.

- **Complaint logs.**
Systematically record all the complaints that arise, how they are handled, and the outcome.

- **Ongoing complaint analysis.**
Use the information from the logs to put in place continuous improvement systems for error detection and prevention.

- **Brainstorming for zero-defect standards.**
Conduct periodic meetings with employees about reducing errors, steps, costs, and contact points.

- **Complaint case studies for universal examination.**
Circulate customers' complaints for employee review and comment so that all are aware of the issues, the appropriate resolution, and prevention techniques. Use them as training tools at staff meetings.

- **Benchmarking.**
Find out what world-class leaders in any industry do and copy them.

SWIM

Once in a while you will find both you and your customer stumped by a problem with no apparent solution. Often these challenges seem to lie in the technology that many of us use, but few of us understand.

A long distance operator and her customer had struggled hopelessly to complete a call. Finally, with a frustrated sigh, she said, "Sir, you and I have been trying to make that credit card work on every long distance carrier in existence. I can't figure out what's wrong or why they won't accept it. I'll place the call for you and we'll call it even. No charge!"

Knowing and exercising the authority you have to extend small courtesies can provide you with an escape from the sinkhole of futile actions.

PLAN OF ACTION		
The three most important ideas I gained from this section:	*I intend to use this idea when my customer/my boss/I/other:*	*When I applied this idea the result was:*
Date 1.		*Date*
Date 2.		*Date*
Date 3.		*Date*

Chapter 5

Exposure Recovery

Mistakes *do* occur. People do foul up. Systems do break down. Sometimes customers do it and sometimes we do it. We put them on hold, we transfer them, we ignore them. They get mad. How your company handles the recovery opportunities can set you apart from all the others in the business. The true test of quality and excellence (from the customer's point of view) comes at the time of maximum exposure, when you are stripped bare, when they do not get what they expected. It is this moment that can pay off in customers for life or costs so enormous your company may not survive.

> ✓ *Checklist*
> **Exposure**
> **Recovery**
> ❑ *Recovery process*
> ❑ *Sentence maps*

The Recovery Process

Once a complaint surfaces:

- Devote your complete attention to the customer.

- Take all the time necessary.

- Eliminate all distractions and interruptions.

- Take notes.

- Use the Complaint Management Model shown on page 9.

- Familiarize yourself with Sentence Maps on page 39.

- Use the Exposure Recovery Scripts beginning on page 50.

✓ *Checklist*
Recovery Process

❑ *Devote your complete attention to the customer*

❑ *Take all the time necessary*

❑ *Eliminate all distractions and interruptions*

❑ *Take notes*

❑ *Use the Complaint Management Model*

❑ *Familiarize yourself with Sentence Maps*

❑ *Use the Exposure Recovery Scripts*

SINK

If you ignore a customer, it may result in a complaint or in a lost sale. Customers expect you to take them seriously whether it's a complaint, an inquiry, or a request for information.

Several years ago I decided to move my office to a location more representative of my business, one that would distinguish my work from others. I talked to real estate agents, colleagues, and clients. For a brief time I seriously considered relocating to a boat in the marina situated in the heart of the city. I gave up that idea when the boat dealers offered only token assistance. Several months later I had this conversation with one of them:

"I heard you bought a marina condominium for your office— and paid cash for it too," the dealer said. "You're right," I answered. "I thought you were going to buy a boat from us and put your office in that," he commented. "I was," I answered, "but you never gave me a call." His response? "We really didn't think you meant it."

The consumer world gossips about the poorly dressed but wealthy man who withdrew his millions from the bank when the clerk treated him badly. When you jump to a conclusion about a customer, it can be business-life threatening.

Sentence Maps

Sentence maps are useful phrases designed to clarify your client's thoughts, express your understanding of her need, and empathize with his position. They are tools to help you keep on target with your clients. Properly applied and with appropriate sensitivity, when you use these phrases, you will find your client doing most of the "work" for you. Each sentence map is marked with a diamond (♦). Familiarize yourself with each one, try it, and rework it until it fits for you.

SWIM

Most companies want their customers to know that they really care about them. It can be a challenge to set yourself apart from your competitors and show that your customers have special meaning.

Many years ago, before I founded Milestone Unlimited, I began adding to my vacation "wish-you-were-here" card list the names of important business contacts. I continue that practice today: if I'm on any extended trip (more than three days), my clients can count on getting at least one postcard. The cost is small but the results are big. Some have even started sending me cards when they travel!

"Our employees really like it when you send us postcards," a CEO mentioned during one of our meetings. "None of us gets much chance to travel and it's good to see the sights even if it's only on paper and through our consultant's eyes."

Small thoughtful gestures reduce the sharp edges of mistakes that can destroy a hard-won relationship.

Open-Ended Questions

These questions usually begin with *who, what, where, when,* and *how.* They cannot be answered by *yes* or *no.* They give you information about the client's point of view.

◆ How did this whole thing start?

◆ Can you tell me what happened?

◆ How did you expect it to be handled?

◆ What is it about...?

Example:

Client: The deductible is wrong.

You: What is it about the *DEDUCTIBLE** that's wrong?

*When using these words, substitute your words for those in capital letters.

SINK

You are the expert in your job. You probably know more than your customer does in most of the technical aspects. You tread dangerous water, however, when you contradict your customer's personal experience—he or she is the expert.

The airline passenger, the CEO of one of my client companies, became increasingly uncomfortable as the cabin temperature climbed higher and higher.

"Is it just me?" he asked his seatmate, "or is it getting warmer in here?" The other traveler agreed with his observation so the CEO spoke to the flight attendant. Arrogantly she responded, "Sir, you can't be too warm. The overhead airflow valve is open all the way." As she turned away, the captain's voice came over the speaker, "Ladies and gentlemen, we know that some of you are getting a little warm back there. We'll have it adjusted in just a moment."

Feel free to assert the facts, if you must. Forego the need to dispute the customer's feelings.

SWIM

Because of the nature and complexity of their business, there are enterprises whose mistakes become almost bigger than life. The more business you have, the more mistakes you make. Your occupation becomes a source of media jokes. If you can acknowledge errors gracefully and without prompting, and correct them on the spot, you can head off serious consequences.

For several days I had received no mail—not an ad, not a catalog, not a bill. This was highly unusual, so I phoned the post office to inquire. Based on the publicity the postal service had received, I expected the worst. Instead, this is what I heard.

"It looks to me like your mail got held by mistake when your address got confused with your neighbor who went on vacation last week," said the post office rep. "It was our error, no doubt about it. We'll send someone over with your mail within the half hour or whenever it's convenient for you."

Clarifying Responses

Clarifying responses give you more depth, provide focus, and assure the client you understand both his feelings and the facts. They tell him you were indeed listening. If you are wrong about either the facts or the feelings, he will correct the information, thus helping you avoid solving the wrong problem. By using this format, you can zero in on the critical issue to be resolved.

♦ You sound pretty *DISAPPOINTED* with *THE RESULTS.**

♦ Then you feel that *THE INSTRUCTIONS ARE MISLEADING.**

♦ As I understand it, your need for _____ is *SO URGENT YOU NEED AN IMMEDIATE ANSWER ABOUT YOUR ELIGIBILITY.**

♦ What you're saying then is that *THE PROCEDURES WERE NOT ADEQUATELY EXPLAINED AND YOU'RE NOT SURE WHAT TO DO NOW TO AVOID BEING SENT TO A COLLECTION AGENCY.** Do I have that right?

♦ Looks to me like you're pretty frustrated with the way your complaint was handled.

◆ Okay, now let's see if I have this straight. Your biggest concern is with the discrepancy between the information I've given you and previous information you received.

Empathic Responses

These tell the client you are on her side.

◆ It sometimes must seem like all we do is try to make things difficult for you.

◆ It could be that a mistake was made.

◆ I would be *CONCERNED/WORRIED/FRUSTRATED TOO IF I HADN'T HEARD ANYTHING IN THREE WEEKS AND MY CREDIT RATING WAS IN JEOPARDY.**

SINK

It is said that of the customers who stop doing business with a company, 68% of them go elsewhere because they perceive an attitude of indifference. Does this sound like anyone you know?

When a big discount store moved into a small town several years ago, the long-time merchants were angry with their customers who began shopping at the new store. One merchant complained loud and long, "Boy, customers are really fickle. We've been in business in this town for 40 years and when one of these big shot discount guys comes in, customers can't run there fast enough. And all because that outfit delivers—and on Sundays, too, would you believe!"

He also forgot to mention that the discount store kept hours to better fit the hours of the shoppers as well. The discount store never hung a sign on the door that said "back in a few minutes" or "Closed for two weeks: gone hunting." Nor did it ever tell a customer, "I guess if you want it fixed you'll have to take care of it yourself. And, no, we're not gonna order parts for you either."

There are price shoppers and there are convenience shoppers. But there are those who shop where they are treated well and those who shop where they believe someone cares. How many of your customers are doing business with the competition, not because of price, but because of indifference?

Special Situations

◆ Would you run through that again? I want to be sure I understand exactly how it was handled.

◆ Now that you've painted me such a vivid picture, I can sure see why you look at it that way. With a little more information, I may be able to clear it up for you.

◆ I know you're disappointed that we can't do what you've asked. I'm disappointed too. I can suggest an alternative that others have found satisfactory, however.

◆ It's frustrating when you keep hearing that the plan doesn't cover what you need. Tell me again about your situation and maybe between the two of us something will ring a bell.

When the customer is abusive:

◆ I think we've gotten off on the wrong foot. I'd like to stop a moment and then begin again.

◆ It's perfectly understandable that you're angry. I'd like a minute to think how we might best approach this situation so we can get it resolved for you as effectively as we can.

◆ I can see there's nothing I can do to work this out. Would you have any objection if I put you in touch with my supervisor?

◆ When someone swears at me or calls me names, I'm really no good at working things out or getting questions answered. Is there a different way we could handle this?

> ✓ *Checklist*
> **If an apology is in order**
>
> ❑ *Send flowers*
> ❑ *Send candy*
> ❑ *Send a card*
> ❑ *Give a gift certificate*
> ❑ *Give a discount next time*
> ❑ *Send a paperback book related to their business*
> ❑ *Send a donation to a charity in their name*
> ❑ *Give a magazine subscription*

Most client transactions involve several exchanges. The following example describes the progress of one such transaction.

• The client learns his request is still not processed.

Client: How come every time I want something out of you guys all I hear is that you're working on it?

You: I'm really sorry. It sounds like you haven't been getting the service you expected.

Client: Darn right I haven't! After all, I've been a customer here for longer than you are old, little lady. Why does this always happen to me and no one else I know?

You: You sound pretty disappointed. It's disappointing for me, too, when we can't work as quickly as you'd like. Here's what I can do for you...And I'll follow up on it personally. As soon as it's ready, I'll call you. I'll flag your file too so that the others will be aware of the delays. Does that sound okay?

Client: Well, all right. I'm counting on you to keep your word. I wouldn't want to write a letter to anyone, if you know what I mean.

You: Working this all out with you is very important to me, Mr. Client. I don't want you to have to write a letter to anyone. As we agreed, you'll hear from me between one and two tomorrow on the status. And thanks again for being patient. I know it's not easy sometimes.

Client: That's okay. I know it's not your fault. Just take care of it.

SWIM

The horror stories customers relate are never-ending when it comes to some services. But you can offset bad press if you have an unflagging commitment to make life as easy as possible for your customer.

"Our delivery people will phone you to arrange the time to pick up the loaner chair," the customer service rep said. "We don't expect you to hang around and wait till we show up. If 10 A.M. on the dot is what's convenient for you, that's when they'll be there. If 9:30 suits you better, we'll be there then. Whatever works the best for you."

What a surprise when a customer finds you do not fit the mold he or she has come to expect from similar service providers.

PLAN OF ACTION		
The three most important ideas I gained from this section:	*I intend to use this idea when my customer/my boss/I/other:*	*When I applied this idea the result was:*
Date 1.		Date
Date 2.		Date
Date 3.		Date

Chapter 6

Exposure Recovery Scripts

What Do You *Really* Say to the Customer When...

One of the more helpful and time-saving tools you can add to your repertoire of complaint management tools is the building and use of scripts. Many of your complaints will fall into similar patterns for which standard responses can be tailored. When you use just the right combination of words, coupled with a sensitivity to your customer's position, the result will be notable in its impact. The framework or script tells you how and what to say within a defined context. You can then concentrate on the unique aspects of the transaction and customer individuality.

✓ *Checklist*
**Exposure
Recovery
Scripts**
❏ *Four-part empathic
   model*
❏ *Scripts*
❏ *Practice (p. 111)*

Four-Part Empathic Model

When a customer confronts you with a complaint, you want to come up with just the right words. When you can't remember the right words, you can use a basic format and fill in the blanks. The Four-Part Empathic Model that follows establishes you as attentive and creates an effective summary of the transaction.

Empathy → Acknowledgment → Reassurance → Action

Part One: Empathy—To empathize is to identify with and understand another's situation, feelings, and motives *from his point of view.* It's not enough just to understand; you need to speak to him in such a way that he knows you have listened to the specifics. A true breakthrough will come if you can say what he's thinking and feeling better than he can himself.

Part Two: Acknowledgment—To acknowledge is to recognize the validity of his position *from his point of view* and to restate it to his satisfaction.

It is *not* necessary that you agree with either the feelings or the facts *from your point of view.* You are simply acting as a translator.

Part Three: Reassurance—To reassure is to restore your customer's confidence in you and to articulate the benefit to the customer.

Part Four: Action—To act is to do something. It is not enough to empathize, acknowledge, and reassure. The action is what counts.

Build your own scripts by using the Four-Part Empathic Model illustrated in the two examples below.

Example 1:

Empathy	"When you feel you've been given the runaround, I can understand...
Acknowledgment	...your reluctance to talk with me instead of a supervisor.
Reassurance	If you'll give me just a few minutes, though, I think you'll find between the two of us we can work out a satisfactory solution without taking up even more of your time by starting all over with somebody new.
Your action	Now I'm going to run through it again as you explained it to me. Stop me if I don't have it right, and I'll make the adjustment."

Example 2:

Empathy	"You sound pretty disappointed with the information I just told you.
Acknowledgment	Before we give up on your request for _____, however...
Reassurance	...I want to be sure there's nothing I'm aware of that's changed.
Your action	Let me get Mr. Bigg in on this conversation and listen to his ideas about alternatives. I'd be interested in hearing them myself. Do you have any objections to that?"

SINK

"Why don't customers plan better? Why don't they let us know in advance? We could improve our service to them if they wouldn't wait until the last minute to order!" This is a major complaint many of us have about customers. But customers learn quickly that some companies don't seem to care.

Traveling, much as you might enjoy it, can be a major stress producer. The more advance preparation, the better the trip, the better the attitude of the traveler. Ground transportation to the airport is high on the traveler's critical to-do list. It sets the tone not only for that trip, but subsequent ones as well.

Listen in on this traveler's complaint to the owner of the cab company: "I just thought you might want to know—today was the second time your dispatch agent talked me into making an advance reservation to have a taxi pick me to go to the airport. It's also the second time they've never shown up. I don't like starting my trips in a panic and mad besides! I had to flag down a passing cab and I just want you to know I'll never use your company again!"

Without dedicated follow-through by the company, the customer who plans soon becomes discouraged and joins those who wait until the last moment. Or they complain, or they go to the competition. And they have decided it's fruitless to plan or to give you advance warning.

Scripts

The rest of this section contains ready-made scripts—ready-to-use examples—of the most common situations that create unhappy customers. All came from written cases described by participants in customer service seminars.

The format defines, answers, and clarifies the most frequent questions asked by those in the trenches with the unhappy customer— "What do you *really* say to the customer when...?"

The structure of each case illustration includes:

◆ **Title:** The type of situation.

◆ **Situation:** Description of a typical transaction.

◆ **What you say:** Suggested scripts answering the question, "What should you *really* say?"

◆ **Why this works:** Explanation of the rationale for the choice of response.

◆ **Tip:** Many of these scripts contain helpful hints to help you through the situation.

◆ **Key elements:** Generic steps to follow whenever this type of situation arises.

What Do You Really Say to the Customer When...

1. All The Phones Ring At Once

◆ **Situation**: Three lines are ringing and you're the only one there to manage the incoming calls.

◆ **What you say**: "XYZ Company, please hold."

OR

"XYZ Company, will you please hold?" (Wait for the customer's response and act accordingly.)

OR

"XYZ Company, I'll be with you in just a moment. Can you hold?" (Again, wait for the customer's response and act accordingly.)

◆ **Why this works**: "Please hold" gives you total control of the situation and allows you to proceed with the incoming phone calls. "Will you please hold?" asks permission. This begins a two-way communication process between you and your customer that can further the problem-solving process.

◆ **Tip**: Don't ask a question—"Will you please hold...?"—unless you intend to let the customer answer.

◆ **Key elements**:
- Smile, give your company's name.
- Decide how much control to allow the caller.

2. On-Hold Is A Chronic Condition

◆ **Situation**: Because of staff shortage, your customer has been on hold for an unreasonable amount of time. She is a frequent buyer and needs to call in often to talk with you. Waiting on hold seems to have become a way of life for her.

◆ **What you say**: "Mrs. Smith, you probably feel like over time you've been on hold long enough to have written a book. Let's see what I can do to get this situation taken care of immediately to get you on your way."

◆ **Why this works**: The empathic statement ("you probably feel...") acknowledges that you understand her frustration. It lightens up the dialogue and tells her you intend to proceed rapidly so that she can get on with her business.

◆ **Key elements**:
  • Know your system's shortcomings.
  • Acknowledge the customer's feelings.
  • Take charge.
  • Begin problem-solving immediately.

3. You're Face-To-Face With A Customer And The Phone Rings

◆ **Situation**: A customer approaches your desk and the phone rings shortly thereafter.

◆ **What you say**: "Mr. Customer, excuse me just a moment while I answer the phone."

OR

"Mr. Customer, can you wait while I answer the phone?" Then to the caller, "Mr. Caller, I'm with a customer. I'll phone you back within the hour or you can call me back. Which do you prefer?"

◆ **Why this works**: The person who is there first, according to the ways of our society, takes precedent. If you give preference to the customer who phones, you create a barrier between you and the walk-in customer. This is particularly critical when the walk-in customer has taken his time to physically come to you.

Give the caller a specific time when you will return the call. This appointment will alleviate two potential problems: (1) the caller sitting by the phone as a prisoner waiting for you to call, and (2) the caller phoning you back again when it's inconvenient for you. If the caller says it's an emergency, ask permission from your walk-in customer: "This is an emergency. Would you mind waiting?" If he says "yes, I mind," you are bound to take care of him first.

◆ **Tip**: When a walk-in customer approaches, notify the switchboard to transfer your calls to someone else so they will not divert your attention.

◆ **Key elements**:

- First come, first served.
- Ask permission of your walk-in customer.
- Make a call-back appointment with your phone caller.

4. Co-Worker Does Not Return Phone Calls

◆ **Situation**: A customer has phoned several times this week, leaving messages each time for your co-worker to call back. The co-worker has not returned any of the calls. The customer now is talking with you and is very angry.

◆ **What you say:** "Mr. Smith, I'm sorry you have been inconvenienced by this matter. If you give me a little background, perhaps I can help you."

OR

"Mr. Smith, I'm sorry you've been inconvenienced. Would you like to speak with anyone else, perhaps Mrs. Jones, the supervisor?"

OR A COMBINATION

"Mr. Smith, I'm sorry you've been inconvenienced. I can leave another message, perhaps I can help you, or you can talk with Mrs. Jones, the supervisor. Which would you prefer?"

◆ **Why this works**: You begin rebuilding the relationship between the customer and the company. You give the customer options. You take responsibility for moving the transaction to some kind of conclusion.

◆ **Key elements**:

- Empathize with the customer's inconvenience.
- Provide alternatives.
- Specify by name and rank the individual who will be talking with the customer in place of your co-worker.

5. Taking A Message For A Nonresponsive Co-Worker

◆ **Situation**: A customer has phoned many times for your co-worker who has not returned the calls. The customer will not talk to the supervisor; he wants *you* to make your co-worker call him.

◆ **What you say**: "Mr. Customer, I'll be happy to let Mr. Co-worker know that you called." (Do not say, "I'll have Mr. Co-worker call you back.")

◆ **Why this works**: It is important that you promise only what you can deliver, which is to give your co-worker the message that a customer has called several times—unless you want to take personal responsibility for making your co-worker return the call. Once you say you will see to it that your co-worker returns the call, the responsibility shifts from your co-worker to you. Unless you are the co-worker's supervisor, this is an inappropriate responsibility for which you have no authority.

◆ **Key elements**:

- Acknowledge the customer's request.
- Promise only what you can deliver.

SWIM

Managing customer attitudes is a significant part of managing customer complaints. Managing the business's attitude toward the customer comes before everything else. You can see it everywhere:

How do you word a customer benefit? On the bottom of a restaurant menu:

"Substitutions gladly, of course"

How do you word a letter of apology? From a letter received in response to a customer complaint: "Thank you for caring enough about our company to write. We have fallen short of expectations, both yours and ours. Our intent is to re-establish your confidence in us so that you will not hesitate to recommend us to any of your associates. We are sending you three...We realize we must behave our way out of the problem we have created and would like to know if there is anything else we can do to make this up to you. Please don't hesitate to call me and let me know."

How do you word a "Do not ..." warning to a customer? From a tent card found in a hotel room: "Would we make you lug your towel every time you leave your room for a swim? Absolutely not. Would we build a pool and not stock it with towels? Of course not. Some guests actually think they have to take the towels from their rooms to the pool. Can you imagine that? We ask you to strike at the heart of this inaccurate assumption. Simply leave the towels in your room and get one from the stand by the pool."

6. Follow-Through Fails

◆ **Situation**: Your co-worker makes a commitment to a customer to resolve a problem but does not follow-through. The customer comes in expecting the problem to be resolved. Your co-worker has the day off. You must work with the customer.

◆ **What you say**: "Mr. Customer, I know how frustrating it is when you expect something to be done and it isn't. Let's see what I can do about it. As I understand it, your request was..."

OR

"It's frustrating...While I have some notes here about your concern, Mr. Customer, it would help me if you would go over the matter again so that I know I'm on the right track."

◆ **Why this works**: You acknowledge the feeling state of the customer and share it with him, which puts both of you on the same side of the problem without blaming your co-worker. You move immediately into problem-solving by restating the information you have for clarification. By asking the customer to confirm your information, it gets him to listen. By asking him to restate his concern, it allows you to clarify and to assess his level of distress.

◆ **Key elements**:

- Empathize with the customer.
- Clarify the information.
- Take action.

7. Backlog Hampers Handling

◆ **Situation**: The previous person in your job left a backlog of orders and very upset customers because he did not complete the work. As a result, you must redo some of it, which further inconveniences the customer.

◆ **What you say**: "Mr. Customer, I would like to introduce myself. I am Joe Smith and I am replacing Harry Jones with whom you

worked earlier. In the process of personnel shifts, there may have been some inquiries that slipped through the cracks. I'd like to go over the information I have to confirm its accuracy and to let you know the status of your request. This may take a few minutes and it may mean redoing some things that you've already done. But it's important to me personally that you and I get off on the right track and that everything is as smooth as it can be in the future."

◆ **Why this works**: It briefly explains the reason for the clarification. It introduces you in such a way that you can establish a relationship of problem-solving and a reputation of careful checking. It avoids blaming the irresponsible co-worker and does not put your company in a bad light because this was allowed to happen.

◆ **Key elements**:

- Explain the personnel change.
- Clarify the information needed.
- Assure the customer that you personally are on top of the situation and will take action.

8. Information Unavailable When Promised

◆ **Situation**: Your customer called with a specific request, but you did not have the information immediately available. You assured the customer you would get the information and call him within a specified time. However, you were unable to get the information by the time you promised.

◆ **What you say**: "Mr. Customer (call him back at the time you promised), because I haven't run into this before, it's taking me a little bit longer to get the information you requested. I've made it number one on my priority list. I'd like to promise you that I'll have exactly what you need by tomorrow afternoon,

but I'm not sure I can do that. What I will do is call you back tomorrow between 3:00 and 4:00 and let you know the status. How does that sound?"

◆ It briefly explains to the customer the delay, and assures him that you're taking personal responsibility and not putting him off. It enables you to proceed without making a promise you cannot keep.

◆ **Key elements**:

- Acknowledge the difficulty.
- Make a personal commitment.
- Allow for a possible continued delay.

9. Supervisor Intervention Is Requested

◆ **Situation**: The customer received the wrong material. You apologized and explained you would pay the freight on another shipment. Your customer calls a week later; he still has not received the material. The shipping department promises they will get the material out next week, which you tell the customer, who now demands to speak to your supervisor.

◆ **What you say**: "Mr. Customer, I think that's a good idea. I'll get my supervisor on the phone with us and see if there's anything she can do. (Get your supervisor on the phone for a three-way conversation with you and the customer). Mrs. Supervisor, I have Mr. Customer on the phone with me now. (Explain to the supervisor what has occurred.) Mr. Customer has asked to speak with you about this. I agreed it was appropriate to see if there are any other options or what we might do to assure him that, indeed, the shipment will be on his doorstep when Shipping says it will."

◆ **Why this works**: You have done everything you can do within the scope of your job and your authority. By figuratively going with your customer to the supervisor, you strengthen your relationship, continue the trust-building process, and show the customer you will do whatever it takes to see to it that the problem is resolved.

◆ **Key elements**:

- Acknowledge the legitimacy of the customer's request.
- Escalate to a level where the problem can be resolved.
- Keep control of the request.

SINK

Customers want to believe a company's advertising. They want to trust the words of the personnel. They want to take things at face value. They don't want to interpret; they don't want to be suspicious and skeptical. And yet...they learn.

What did the travel agency client learn after she discovered, too late, that a fare cheaper than hers, existed?

"I know we say that we'll get you the lowest airline fare," the agent acknowledged. "But we meant at the time you place your order. It's the customer's responsibility to watch the newspapers, see if there are lower rates, and then call us if there's a better deal."

Avoid misleading the customer. If there is fine print, in policy or in practice, disclose it.

10. Careless Co-Worker Mishandles Customer Transaction

◆ **Situation**: You and several other employees do the same job. A customer complains to you about a co-worker who constantly mishandles the work.

◆ **What you say**: "Mr. Customer, I know how difficult it is when you expect something to happen and it doesn't go the way you want. In the future when you call, if you ask for me directly, I can see to it that your request is handled appropriately."

◆ **Why this works**: This statement reflects your understanding of your customer's position, gives him an alternative he can count on, and focuses on the transaction rather than on your co-worker.

◆ **Tip**: You need to bring to your boss's attention the errors created by your careless co-worker. If you do not, the errors of the co-worker will continue to occur and they may continue entangling you.

◆ **Key elements**:

- Acknowledge the customer's concern.
- Set the performance standard.
- Provide your customer with an alternative for future reference.

11. Delay Occurs—Another Department

◆ **Situation**: You must tell your customer the bad news that Shipping has delayed her order for the third time even though you had given her a firm delivery commitment only yesterday.

◆ **What you say**: "Mrs. Customer, I wanted to let you know just as soon as I received the information. The shipment I said would arrive tomorrow is going to be further delayed. I know this will cause you some inconvenience. Shipping *has* given me a new date and they assure me it will arrive for sure at that time. I want you to know that I'll follow up on your order personally. In the meantime, I can pursue getting you a partial shipment if that would help. Would you like me to see what I can do about that?"

◆ **Why this works**: You call the customer immediately upon receiving the information, which assures her that you are taking care of her interests. You reinforce that you will be taking personal responsibility for tracking the item. You show your concern for her well-being by presenting her with alternatives that may tide her over until the complete order arrives.

◆ **Tip**: Call the customer first—before she calls you.

◆ **Key elements**:

- Inform the customer immediately of the delay.
- Take personal responsibility for follow-up.
- Offer an alternative that you can deliver on.

12. Delay Occurs—Your Vendor

◆ **Situation**: Your customer places an order. You agree to a delivery date. Your customer arrives to pick up her purchase, but your vendor has failed to deliver.

◆ **What you say**: "Mrs. Customer, your order is not here as we agreed it would be. I've put a tracer on it to see what's happened and to get some idea of when we can expect it. On behalf of the company I want to extend our apologies for the inconvenience this has caused you. What can we do to help you now?"

◆ **Why this works**: You have acknowledged the error and the inconvenience it has created for the customer. You have told her what you are doing about it, assuring her that you will let her know when she can expect what she requested. By asking her how you should proceed, you open the door for two-way communication, which moves the transaction into a mutual problem-solving mode. Until you know the extent of the inconvenience the delay has created for your customer, it is inappropriate and a waste of time to offer specific alternatives.

◆ **Tip**: You'll save your customer an unnecessary trip if you institute an early warning system, i.e., a tickler file reminder of pending orders, to alert you to delayed deliveries.

◆ **Key elements**:

- Acknowledge the problem.
- Confirm your next action.
- Ask the customer's opinion.

13. Delay Occurs— Customer's Vendor

◆ **Situation**: The customer placed an order and asked that you ship it through his vendor. It has not arrived. Your records show it has been shipped and you believe the lack of follow-through is the error of your customer's vendor.

◆ **What you say**: "Mr. Customer, our records show the order was shipped via your vendor on June first. If you could check with your shipper and send me your paperwork, I'll be glad to double check it on our end."

◆ **Why this works**: You acknowledge the lack of delivery. You give the customer a route to follow. You do not take responsibility for the failure of your customer's vendor. By suggesting that once he checks on his end you will follow-up on yours, you have room for resolving the mix-up without placing blame. If you tell the customer it is his vendor's fault and not yours, you imply that the customer is at fault for selecting an inappropriate vendor.

◆ **Tip**: Fix the problem; don't fix blame.

◆ **Key elements**:

- Clarify without blaming.
- Refer the customer to his vendor.
- Provide a life line for follow-up.

14. Equipment Is Unreliable

◆ **Situation**: Your customer complains of repeated equipment failures. He worries about equipment reliability and the possibility of latent defects.

◆ **What you say**: "Mr. Customer, I can understand how concerned you must be that what has already happened several times will continue. I, too, would want to know what to do to guard against possible future failures. We're concerned, too, about the trouble you had with the installed equipment. We'd like to work with you to determine what's going on. Here's how we may be able to help." (Offer options: a trouble shooter, replacements, etc.)

OR

"Mr. Customer, I can understand your concern about the failures you are experiencing. We, too, are concerned about it. What is it that you would like us to do?"

◆ **Why this works**: You empathize with the customer's position, the frustration, and perhaps additional costs he is experiencing. You acknowledge that this also worries you and that your company is not ignoring it. With a ready plan in place, i.e., replacement parts or a site visit, you demonstrate your active role in resolving the problem. If this is new knowledge to you about equipment performance, your question to the customer about his ideas will give you the opportunity to hear what thoughts he has given to it. It makes this a mutual problem-solving approach.

◆ **Tip**: At the first sign of a recurring product failure, alert your boss, so it can be addressed immediately.

◆ **Key elements**:

- Empathize with the customer.
- State your company's equal concern.
- Present a plan of action.
- Ask for the customer's thoughts.

15. Error Results In Overcharge

◆ **Situation**: Your customer is very upset because a company error has resulted in an additional charge to her account.

◆ **What you say**: "Mr. Customer, I can understand how upset you are that these additional charges have shown up because of our error. I'd be upset too. Here's what I can do about it."

◆ **Why this works**: It's important when you have an upset customer that you acknowledge and restate her concern. This shows you have been listening, that you understand, and that you are personally interested in getting it resolved. That you can immediately offer a way of rectifying the situation also demonstrates to your customer you are a knowledgeable person who has the authority to act.

◆ **Tip**: You need to know the standard procedures for correcting organizational errors and the scope of authority you have to take action.

◆ **Key elements**:

- Empathize with the customer.
- Express your similar feeling.
- Correct the error.

16. Chronic Product Failure Occurs

◆ **Situation**: Five of the last 200 units shipped to your customer failed. He wants to know what you are going to do.

◆ **What you say**: "Mr. Customer, I'm glad you brought this to our attention immediately. I'll get our engineer on the phone with us. I'd like you to explain the details to him so that we can get on this right away. Do you have time to discuss this with John Smith now or is there someone more familiar with the breakdown who can discuss the technical aspects of it?"

◆ **Why this works**: When you thank customers for alerting you immediately, you set the stage for them to bring concerns to you without delay in the future. When you bring the expert into a joint conversation, you demonstrate a sincere and professional interest in resolving the concern immediately. When you ask if he has a more qualified person available, it allows your customer to think about the most knowledgeable person to include. Because the discussion may be lengthy, it's important to verify that it is a convenient time.

◆ **Tip**: Know your expert's name so that you can personalize the action.

◆ **Key elements**:

- Thank your customer.
- Act on it immediately.
- Connect your expert with your customer.
- Determine timing.
- Provide the opportunity for technician-to-technician talk.

SWIM

Have you ever met the gremlin that hides out in the copy machine and inserts errors into previously perfect copy? No matter how often I proofread my material before taking it to the printer, an error inevitably appears.

When I reread the flyer, announcing an upcoming seminar, I discovered a significant mistake in the copy. And 135 of those darned things filled the box sitting on the counter! And I knew the reprint costs would exceed my budget.

My disappointed groan alerted the print shop owner. "If you want to retype it, I'll be happy to rerun it again no charge," he said. "But it was my error," I said. "Yes, I know the error in your copy was a typographic one," he said, "but the rule here at our print shop is that we'll rerun your job free if you want to retype your copy and you have fewer than 200 copies."

What could ensure loyalty more than a business partner who will bail you out of a jam? What could delight a customer more?

17. Control Is Out Of Your Hands

◆ **Situation**: Your customer is waiting for a resolution to his problem, but a labor strike stands in the way of success.

◆ **What you say**: "Mr. Customer, I'm frustrated, too, that we have to wait to get this fixed. While I can't predict when the strike will be settled, I can see to it that within 24 hours of the settlement your order will be out the door and on its way. I'll call you to let you know when I've taken that action. Does that make sense to you?"

◆ **Why this works**: It acknowledges the frustration you both share about something beyond your control; success for both of you hinges on someone else's action. By presenting a plan of action with very specific, measurable standards of performance, you tell the customer two things: (1) you are aware of the situation and you are taking appropriate steps to assure minimum delay; and (2) it relieves the customer of any further action on his part.

◆ **Tip**: Identify a contact person who will notify you when the strike is settled. Take action immediately.

◆ **Key elements**:

- Empathize with your customer.
- Share your like frustration.
- Prepare a plan to activate upon immediate elimination of the obstacle.
- Get the customer's agreement.

18. Expectations Are Not Met— Product

◆ **Situation**: Because of miscommunication at the point of sale, the customer finds that his system will not work exactly as expected.

◆ **What you say**: "Mr. Customer, I can understand your confusion about the difference between what you expected and what you are now receiving from your system. It sounds like more emphasis should have been placed on that aspect of the application process. How would you like us to proceed?"

OR

"Here are three options. We can put you in touch with one of our other customers who has a similar use to discuss how it works for them. We can send out our technician to train your people in the most effective application of the system as it now exists; that costs about $25 an hour. Or third, we can arrange to install the additional equipment. This third option will require a new contract and is the most expensive of the three options. Which would you be interested in pursuing?"

◆ **Why this works**: This acknowledges the breakdown in communications without blaming either the customer or your company for not nailing down the actual need of the customer satisfactorily. When you present three choices with a range of costs, the customer can examine his budget to decide what is practical. Your customer may come up with another option you may be willing to consider. It opens the transaction for mutual problem-solving.

◆ **Tip**: You need to know the options available when there is a discrepancy between expectations and application. Unless you have full authority, do not quote figures.

◆ **Key elements**:

- Acknowledge the discrepancy without placing blame.
- Present options with cost range.
- Ask your customer's preference.

19. Expectations Are Not Met— Distributor Service

◆ **Situation**: You receive a call from a disappointed consumer who is angry because the product and the service are poor. A dealer distributor provides both.

◆ **What you say**: "Ms. Customer, I'm sorry to hear of your disappointment with the dealer, with our product, and what you have done to resolve it. While we usually don't get involved in matters of this sort, I'll see what we can do and get back to you within the next hour. Is that all right with you?"

◆ **Why this works**: You are standing behind your product. You have not criticized the dealer. You have proposed further investigation. You may be able to do some negotiating between the dealer and your customer or bring in a third party who has the authority to intervene. If you tell the customer it's a problem between her and the dealer, you risk losing the customer's business, current and future, and good public relations for your product.

◆ **Key elements**:

- Acknowledge your customer's experience.
- State the uniqueness of the request.
- Investigate.
- Gain the customer's agreement.

20. Expectations Are Not Met— Repair Time

◆ **Situation**: Your customer brings in a job she believes is relatively simple, i.e., can be completed in less than 30 minutes. The job will take several hours to complete.

◆ **What you say**: "Ms. Customer, two hours does seem like a long time to fix something like this for a person like me who is not an engineer. Our technicians tell me this is one of the most delicate instruments we have and takes more time than what we have been used to in the past. Because you're in a hurry, I'll ask them to put it at the top of their list. They're usually anxious to please, too. I'm not sure it would be wise to do something less than make sure it works the way you want it to, unless you suggest otherwise."

◆ **Why this works**: It acknowledges your customer's inconvenience and attributes it to the quality or sophistication of the equipment. By identifying it as a priority item, you assure the customer she'll be inconvenienced as little as possible. You get her agreement that it's worth the time it takes, unless she authorizes you to cut corners.

◆ **Key elements**:

- Acknowledge the inconvenience.
- Explain briefly the technical nature of the problem.
- Flag for priority treatment.
- Confirm the mutual desire for a quality solution.

21. Expectations Are Not Met— Time Frame

◆ **Situation**: The customer wants an order filled and shipped this week to meet a commitment for one of her customers. You cannot fulfill the request.

◆ **What you say**: "I'd be glad to fill your request on such short notice if we could without jeopardizing the quality you've come to depend on. Like you, I sure don't want to let down a good customer. We could get you a partial shipment or send you a substitute that may suffice. Would either alternative be suitable?"

◆ **Why this works:** You reinforce the integrity of your operation. You recognize that the customer is in a bind, without telling her she was unrealistic in her expectations. By giving some options as the next step, you move into a mutual problem-solving mode. If your company will allow it, you may want, as an alternative, to check with a competitor to find out if they can deliver on your customer's need.

◆ **Tip:** It is to your advantage to act as the go-between if you ask a competitor for assistance.

◆ **Key elements:**

- Educate your customer.
- Reinforce the integrity of your organization.
- Avoid blaming customers for their short-sightedness.
- Offer options.
- Let the customer decide.

22. Solution Requested Is Illegal

◆ **Situation:** You work for a government agency; your customer (the taxpayer) requests an action that is against the law.

◆ **What you say:** "Mr. Customer, I'd be glad to authorize the procedure if the law would allow it. As I understand the law, you might be subject to a substantial fine and a possible jail sentence if you were to proceed in that direction. I can understand how unreasonable it seems. While I'm not aware of anything we can do in this office to change that, I can refer you to the legislator in your district who may have an alternative for you. Would you be interested in having her name?"

◆ **Why this works:** It gives a brief explanation to the taxpayer as to the limitations in the law and the consequences. You acknowledge his feelings and you give him another action he can take. This approach reduces the animosity created when a taxpayer hears, "The law won't allow it. There's nothing I can do about it." If you ask the customer's permission before referring her to another resource, you reduce the impression that you are passing the buck.

◆ **Key elements**:

- Explain briefly the law. (Do not make excuses.)
- Outline briefly the penalties. (Do not dwell on them.)
- Empathize with the customer's position.
- Refer him to someone who can hear his concerns and possibly make a difference
- Ask permission to refer.

SINK

Fair play is a concept that most of us understand instinctively even if we can't spell it out in logical, rational terms. Long-term loyal customers begin to question their loyalty when they believe you value the customer you don't have over the customer you do have.

Any business owner will tell you that the most expensive customer is the one you have to find, the one you have to go after. Yet that same owner will offer the biggest discount, the sign-up bonus, and the come-ons to the prospective customer. Seldom will the customer who does business there day-after-day, year-after-year have the same opportunity.

How fairly treated do you think the customer felt when he heard this? "Yes, I know you've been a regular customer for many years and spent a lot of money here. But this free gift and bargain rate are only for new customers."

When your marketing department offers an incentive to attract a new customer, suggest that it include existing customers in the promotion. A pleasant surprise and a warm letter of appreciation go a long way to reinforce the practice of loyalty.

23. Solution Requested Is Too Costly

◆ **Situation**: Your customer requests your company resolve a problem at a cost too great for your company to manage.

◆ **What you say**: "Mr. Customer, I've explored all the possibilities I can think of to reduce the cost. I had hoped I could come up with a solution that would make economic sense, but I've exhausted all the avenues. I'd be happy to refer you to the manager who can discuss a replacement with you if you're interested"

◆ **Why this works**: You have exercised all your authority, yet still leave the door open for your customer—another option.

◆ **Tip**: Know all pertinent policies in depth.

◆ **Key elements**:

  • Research all possibilities.
  • Explain briefly your limitations.
  • Refer to your supervisor.

24. Customer Demands Co-Worker Firing

◆ **Situation:** Complaining to you about a co-worker, a customer demands that he be fired. He wants to know the outcome.

◆ **What you say**: "Mr. Customer, I'm glad you brought this incident to my attention. I've made careful notes about what occurred and I'm forwarding your concern to Personnel who will investigate. I'd be happy to give you the name of the personnel officer in charge if you would like to follow up on the action taken. Would you like to have her name?"

OR

"Thank you for bringing this matter to my attention. We'll look into it further. I can assure you that this will not happen with your account in the future. The action we'll take with the employee after full investigation is an internal matter. I'm sure you'll agree with me that the most important thing for you is to be sure this does not happen to your account in the future."

◆ **Why this works**: Thanking the customer for bringing this to your attention allows you to save the account and to investigate the matter before anything more serious occurs. While it is in no one's best interest to discuss the outcome of the investigation with a customer (in fact, it may be illegal), it is important to reassure your customer that some action will be taken, that you are not ignoring the event. Once you state the organization's position about its handling of the complaint, returning to problem resolution with the customer focuses attention where it needs to be—on organizational service.

◆ **Tip**: If you have the option, a follow-up letter to acknowledge the customer's complaint (not the request that the individual be fired) is in order here.

◆ **Key elements**:

- Thank the customer.
- Reassure him that action will be taken.
- Safeguard confidentiality.
- Focus on protecting his account.

25. Self-Reliance Fails To Correct A Problem

◆ **Situation**: The customer has been trying to resolve a problem with your equipment on his own for several weeks and has been unable to correct it. He has reached the end of his patience and has called, demanding an immediate answer to the problem.

◆ **What you say**: "Mr. Customer, you must be pretty discouraged by now. I wish I could tell you that there is a simple answer and you'll be up and running within the next 15 minutes. That would be foolish of me and probably a lie. What I can do is get our technician on the phone with us and go over it carefully with him so he can get to work on it right away and get you on your way."

OR

"If I'd been working on this situation as long as you have and still not have it fixed, I'd be pretty upset myself. I wish I could promise you that I could fix it with a simple answer. Before I can give you any estimate of what it will take, however, I need a little more information if you have the time. Are you the one who is most familiar with the problems of the equipment or is there someone else who may have more background?"

◆ **Why this works**: You acknowledged his state of mind and the work he has done. You have begun educating him to a more realistic time frame, stressing your interest in doing it right instead of quickly. Bringing in experts either from your organization or from his to tackle the problem together gives you the best opportunity to correct technical problems and cement relationships for future problem-solving.

◆ **Tip**: Upon resolution of the problem in question, follow up with a phone call to the customer. Suggest that in the future he call your service department at the first sign of trouble.

◆ **Key elements**:

- Acknowledge the customer's work and frustration level.
- Underline the need for quality attention for effective resolution.
- Give a realistic time frame or set of conditions.
- Bring technical experts together with the user.

26. Integrity Of Business Is Questioned

◆ **Situation**: The customer has bought many lottery tickets over the years since the state's games started. He accuses you, as the lottery representative, of rigging it so that no one wins.

◆ **What you say**: "Mr. Customer, I know many people wonder why they haven't won the lottery or know anyone who has. What is it I can do to show you that, indeed, there are winners?"

◆ **Why this works**: It acknowledges the validity of the customer's feelings. It puts the ball back in his court by offering him information if he wants it.

◆ **Tip**: In most instances the customer will not pick up on your offer. He will continue to be upset and suspicious. He hasn't won. He doesn't know anybody who has. There is little you can do that will correct his perception.

◆ **Key elements**:

  • Paraphrase his words.
  • Offer information to counter his belief.

27. Responsibility Is Denied By Customer

◆ **Situation**: Your customer has entered wrong data, but believes it's the fault of your software program.

◆ **What you say:** "Because of the capability of the program you're using, we find that many of our customers have the same experience. Let's see what I can do to help you prevent this from happening again. For your future reference, you'll find this information on page 15 of your manual."

◆ **Why this works**: Although the problems are customer-created errors, it is unnecessary to do battle with her about blame. What is necessary and important is to make the product workable for her quickly and give her a reference point for future need.

◆ **Tip**: Focus on fixing the problem without blame.

◆ **Key elements**:

- Acknowledge your customer's experience and frustration.
- Fix the problem.
- Identify a reference for future use.

28. Invoice Was Not Submitted

◆ **Situation**: Vendor complains he has not received payment for services he completed for your company. He did not send an invoice.

◆ **What you say**: "I'd be unhappy, too, if I hadn't gotten paid yet. I'll be glad to act on it personally if you will send a copy of the invoice directed to my attention. Once I receive it, you can expect payment within two days."

◆ **Why this works**: You acknowledge the worry the vendor has about not being paid. You do not berate him for his error in not sending an invoice. You take personal responsibility, having it directed to your attention, which assures him that a real person will be acting on his behalf. You give him a time frame so he can adjust his records. The time frame will prevent him from calling you daily about his check. When you describe the action needed in a positive manner, you will get the same response and a better relationship than if you had said, "We can't pay your bill until you send an invoice."

◆ **Tip**: Phrase the actions a customer must take in a positive manner. Handle this transaction immediately when you receive the invoice. If you can avoid sending the paperwork through the normal channels so that he can get paid immediately, you will establish a stronger relationship with him and reinforce that it was the lack of invoice that prevented the payment, not that your company is a slow payer. It means you need to have the knowledge to get special treatment for special payments.

◆ **Key elements**:

- Acknowledge your customer's anxiety.
- State in positive terms the action the customer needs to take and the action you will take.
- Give a time frame the customer can count on.

SWIM

When a business or the customer service professional commits to excellence in customer service, cost-free opportunities for delighting your customer spring up.

When I answered the phone one morning, this is what I heard: "Hi, this is Marie at the bank. We're used to seeing your mom come in. We haven't seen her for some time. Since we don't have many customers her age, she's become real special to us. Is she okay?"

Of course, my mom's special to me, too. Her thoughtfulness touched me. How little it takes to personalize an otherwise impersonal relationship. Seek out opportunities to develop meaningful bonds with customers you value.

29. Paperwork Is Incomplete— Instructions Not Followed

◆ **Situation**: Vendor has not received payment because he did not follow the instructions for billing from the purchase order.

◆ **What you say**: "Mr. Vendor, I know the delay in payment has inconvenienced you. If you can help me fill in the information by phone right now, I'll get it down to Accounting right away. In the future, when you send in the purchase order, if you complete lines three and four, your payment will be processed within 24 hours, and you'll have it soon thereafter"

◆ **Why this works**: You acknowledge the concern the vendor has for nonpayment. You act on his complaint immediately to get it processed. You give him the proper procedure to follow by educating him for future action. Reinforce that action by giving him a time frame that will reward him for doing what he needs to do in the appropriate manner.

When customers don't follow your procedure, don't blame them. Don't say, "You should have read the instructions." Fix the problem; don't fix blame. Educate them for the future rather than expect them to be perfect in the past.

◆ **Key elements**:

- Acknowledge the customer's point of view.
- Assist him immediately.
- Fix the problem; don't fix blame.
- Educate the customer for future effective behavior.

30. Service Charge Is "Too High"

◆ **Situation**: The service charge is valid, but the customer doesn't agree with it. She says the bill is too high for the work that was done.

◆ **What you say**: "Mr. Customer, sometimes there is misunderstanding about how we arrive at our charges. I'd be very happy to go over each component with you and how we arrived at the figures. Would you be interested in taking the time to have me clarify the charges?"

◆ **Why this works**: By using the word "misunderstanding," it leaves the door open for both of you to save face in case an error was made by either party. It shows your willingness to take a personal interest in your customer's point of view. If she wants you to explain the details, it will give you the opportunity to explain the values built into the process. It also will give you the chance to discover which part of the charges troubles the customer. You may be able to make some adjustments in the charges if your organization will allow it.

◆ **Key elements**:

  * Use words that allow both you and the customer to save face.
  * Offer a review of each piece of the transaction to clarify the major sensitive area.
  * Adjust charges if allowable.

31. Nothing Satisfies The Customer

◆ **Situation**: The customer appears unsatisfied after you have told her about the available options. She won't choose any of them.

◆ **What you say**: "Mr. Customer, you're disappointed, and you have every right to be. I'm disappointed, too, that we can't come to any resolution of this. What do you suggest we do next?"

◆ **Why this works**: When you have tried everything, or suggested everything you can think of to resolve a customer's concern, and nothing seems acceptable, ask your customer, "From your point of view, what would be the ideal solution?" She may say, "All I really want is an apology." And that you can do.

If the customer asks for something facetious, such as your head on a platter, then you know she's still very angry. Your response at that point is, "If I were in your shoes, Mr. Customer, maybe I'd want the same thing, but then I wouldn't do either one of us much good at getting to the bottom of this. Let's start over from the beginning and see what we can figure out."

◆ **Key elements**:

- Empathize.
- Become a partner with your customer by showing a concern equal to hers.
- Ask for her ideas.

32. Product Is Unavailable

◆ **Situation**: The customer asks for something you are unable to do under any circumstances. For example, you make a product, i.e., lotion found in a hotel bathroom, that is repackaged for a specialized client, an outlet that is not available for the individual customer.

◆ **What you say**: "Mr. Customer, I'm delighted to hear how much you like our product. It's available only through the hotel where you stayed. I would be happy to give you the address of their corporate headquarters, if you would like to write them. Perhaps they could be of help. I'm sure they'd be pleased by your inquiry. Would you be interested in that?"

◆ **Why this works**: The customer is not yours, but she is the customer of your customer. If she is happy with them, they will continue to be customers of yours. While you cannot give her what she wants, she can perhaps get it through your customer. As a side benefit, she will be, in effect, a salesperson for your company if you treat her request seriously and refrain from the standard response of "we're not allowed to do that." You have also given her some action she can take that may pay off for her.

◆ **Tip**: You need to have at your fingertips the addresses of appropriate resources for referral.

◆ **Key elements**:

- Acknowledge the customer's interest in your product.
- Explain briefly your limitations.
- Give her an option she can pursue.

SINK

Young people with little money to spend become grown-ups with lots of money to spend. And most have parents who work hard to instill in them a sense of honor and doing right. It is the short-sighted merchant who forgets that.

In my neighborhood, there is a small gift shop that specializes in unique and expensive one-of-a-kind treasures. My 17 year old son stopped by the shop to pick up the birthday gift I had previously selected for my husband.

"Could you validate my parking?" he asked after he completed the transaction. "Absolutely not!" replied the owner. "Even though you did spend $75 here, I'm not going to validate your parking. You live close enough; you could have walked."

The obvious outcome of bungling a transaction with anyone regardless of age is the risk of not only alienating that individual forever, but also his or her associates. In addition, some researchers have noted that shoplifting and vandalism occur more frequently in those businesses known to mishandle young people.

33. Personalities Conflict

◆ **Situation**: A personality conflict seems to exist between you and your customer. He throws up a mental block when he's dealing with you. You can't break through that barrier no matter what you try.

◆ **What you say**: "Mr. Customer, we seem to have run into a dead-end here. I'm not sure how to proceed. What do you suggest?"

◆ **Why this works**: When you run into a seemingly impossible situation to resolve, it generally means you did not spend enough time with the customer in the discovery stage and options were presented too quickly. The customer still has something on his mind that you have not fully addressed.

By getting him to revisit the issue, it will help identify the areas you need to tackle.

◆ **Tip**: You need to be very objective and control your tone of voice. If you have worked hard to achieve an acceptable result, your frustration and increasing impatience may show through, unless you exercise significant self-discipline.

◆ **Key elements**:

  • Label the roadblock for both you and the customer.
  • Ask for your customer's help.

34. You Have No Authority To Act

◆ **Situation**: Your customer informs you very angrily that she will not accept your solution. She instead suggests an alternative you cannot provide.

◆ **What you say**: "Mr. Customer, I hadn't thought about that as an option. Let's get my supervisor here with us and see if that's something we can pursue."

◆ **Tip**: It is important for you to take her suggestion seriously and to pursue it with her to the next highest level. If your supervisor decides to okay the request, say to the customer, "Mr. Customer, I'm glad you brought that to my attention. I didn't know we could do that. We both learned something today."

◆ **Key elements**:

- Accept the request at face value.
- Escalate to the next highest level—keeping the customer with you.
- Explain the situation to your supervisor.
- Acknowledge courteously your customer's contribution.

SWIM

The creative professional can be a godsend to the customer who finds herself in a situation with few resources.

The plane was hours delayed, no food was served; I was hungry and tired when I finally arrived at the hotel after midnight. Then I discovered that the kitchen was closed. That didn't stop the night clerk, however.

"It's gotta be a real bummer when your plane's so late and you don't get anything to eat," he empathized. "Sorry our restaurant's closed. We don't get many check-ins this late at night. But I'll tell you what—I'll be off duty in 15 minutes. I'll see what I can rustle up in the kitchen if you don't mind plain cheese and crackers. You go on to your room and I'll bring up whatever I can find."

Not only did he find cheese and crackers, he brought an apple and a small candy bar!

When you go out of your way to attend to the comfort of your customer, particularly when the dilemma she faces is not of your making, she will remember what you did for many months, perhaps years. Again, little cost, but big payback.

35. You Are Accused Of Being Rude

◆ **Situation:** Your customer wants you to change your computer billing system. When you explain that it can't be done, she ignores your explanation and accuses you of being rude.

◆ **What you say:** "Ms. Customer, I'm truly sorry you feel I'm being rude. I really do want your business. Can you tell me what I've done to give you that impression?"

◆ **Why this works:** When a customer personalizes a complaint and it seems too obvious to overlook, follow up on it. She will tell you what you did that offends her or will skirt the subject and return to the problem at hand.

◆ **Tip:** Avoid this strategy if you tend to be defensive. It takes particular maturity to remain objective when one feels attacked.

◆ **Key elements:**

- Acknowledge her feeling.
- Apologize for the customer's perception.
- Ask for information.

36. Customer Resists Changes In How You Apply The Company Policy

◆ **Situation:** Your customer has been receiving atypical treatment from your company and now resists conforming to the established company policies printed in the catalog.

◆ **What you say:** "I see the discrepancy you've pointed out, Ms. Customer. You're a valuable customer and we'd like to keep your business, so what I'd like to do is continue our past arrangement with you for this order and your next as you expected. Beginning with the following month's order [give the approximate date], the catalog procedures would then apply. Will that give you enough time to make the adjustments in your procedures?"

- **Why this works:** You are firm about the need to adjust, yet still mindful of the customer's well-being.

- **Tip:** When you discover inconsistencies in how customers are treated, look for ways to blend the current practices into the preferred.

- **Key elements:**

  - Acknowledge the customer's valid distress and confusion.
  - Reinforce the customer's value to the company.
  - Create a transition plan.
  - Gain acceptance.

37. Exceptional Payment Treatment Is Requested

- **Situation:** Customers must pay in advance before you can package and ship their orders. Most have no problem with this, but one constantly orders too late to get her merchandise in a timely manner. "Why don't you believe me when I say our check is in the mail?" she asks when she complains again about the late shipment.

- **What you say:** "Ms. Customer, we could eliminate many of the headaches you're having with this ordering system if we would set up a new procedure for you. I've done some analysis of your buying patterns and have some ideas. Do you have time now to go over these? I think they'd make a real difference and smooth out the bumps for both of us."

- **Why this works:** You are more likely than your customer to find a workable solution, and by noting that you share with her a common annoyance, you reinforce the partnership.

- **Tip:** When there are repetitive complaints from loyal customers it's important to take the time to devise a means of maintaining the relationship if the procedure cannot be changed.

◆ **Key elements:**

- Create a link between the stressful issue and a solution.
- Show your commitment.
- Emphasize your mutual interests.
- Suggest a remedy.

38. Exceptional Credit Preference Is Requested

◆ **Situation:** Your customer's electric power has been disconnected twice for nonpayment. Company policy requires a deposit after two disconnects within a twelve month period. She complains, "How can I pay a deposit when I can't even pay my bill?"

◆ **What you say:** "Ms. Customer, when we spoke about the non-pay last time, I said we stood ready to help you any way we could and you agreed to the arrangement we made then. I wish I could do something else now, but I've gone as far as I can. If I did anything else it would have to come out of my own pocket. I can give you the name of some service agencies for you to contact if you need to make financial arrangements to get your power turned back on. Shall I write them down for you?"

◆ **Why this works:** It restates the agreement without blaming, offers a possible solution, and still leaves the responsibility with the customer.

◆ **Tip:** Avoid being diverted by a seemingly logical question ("how can I pay a deposit...?").

◆ **Key elements:**

- Restate the agreement.
- Describe the boundaries or limitations.
- Inform the customer about possible resources.

SINK

Many changes have occurred in our society over the last 20 years. Not only do merchants need to stay ahead of the competition, they also need to keep up with changing attitudes, factoring these into the way they do business.

The public's stance toward drinking is one of those changing attitudes, resulting in far stricter laws. Establishments offer free taxi-rides home for their patrons and special awards to the nondrinkers to support the efforts to reduce drunken driving and also, of course, to maintain their business. One such enterprise did not get the word.

A group of four people ordered a round of drinks at a local nightclub. The designated driver, who announced he was just that, asked for water. When the bill arrived, a surprise awaited the group.

"I can't believe you'd do this!" exclaimed the young man as he looked over the bill. "I'm the designated driver and I've brought three friends here so they could drink a little. You're charging me $3.50 for every glass of water I drink?"

The exchange became heated, the nondrinking customer was bounced from the club, and a local journalist reported the incident. While we know there are costs associated with serving nondrinkers, few readers sympathized with the business owner.

Changing societal conditions can cost you money. But when you don't change with the times, when you don't adapt to prevalent public notions, you can place your business's future in jeopardy.

39. Delivery Preference Is Requested

◆ **Situation:** Your customer is dissatisfied with the truck loading/ unloading service times at your terminal. He would like to have immediate service when his trucks arrive.

◆ **What you say:** "Mr. Customer, I know how important it is to get your trucks in and out of here as quickly as possible. Normally we unload the trucks as they arrive. However, we'd be happy to work with scheduling you if you would let us know in advance when you expect your trucks to arrive. I've got some thoughts about how that can work out when you have some time to go into it. What would be a convenient time?"

◆ **Why this works:** Both of you get what you want and it also demonstrates your willingness to seek out feasible solutions.

◆ **Tip:** When a customer appears to be more time conscious than most (or has a unique need), incorporate that circumstance in your recommendation.

◆ **Key elements:**

- Summarize your customer's position and your business practice.
- Present a plan you can live with.
- Arrange for a special time to iron out the details.
- Press for a specific next step.

40. Manual Instructions Are Requested

◆ **Situation:** "Where does it say that in the manual!?" your customer complains. He can't find the information that he needs in the manual because (1) he doesn't know where to look, a potential embarrassment to him; (2) it was inadvertently omitted, an embarrassment to the company; or (3) it's "common sense" knowledge, which assumes a more sophisticated customer.

◆ **What you say:** "I can see the problem you're dealing with here. What have you tried?"

◆ **Why this works:** Focusing on the effort already expended will get you swiftly past the criticism and toward a quick end to the predicament.

◆ **Tip:** Note your customer's misinterpretation and follow up internally if your findings have merit.

◆ **Key elements:**

- Recognize your customer's frustration.
- Get the particulars of the pivotal problem.
- Use your customer's efforts as your building base.

41. Problem Is Misdiagnosed Because Of Overconfidence

◆ **Situation:** You do exactly what your customer asks because all her instructions make sense. It turns out that she didn't know what she was talking about, and only thought she did.

◆ **What you say:** "What a bummer it doesn't work like you thought it would, and after all the research you put into it too! We might be able to salvage part of your investment. If you give me about 15 minutes to do an analysis, I can tell you what a new set-up will cost you. Would like me to give it a shot?"

◆ **Why this works:** Right from the beginning of your conversation, you need to leave the responsibility with the customer. If she balks at the mention of cost, you can change your direction. The question at the end directs the focus toward action, not on the past.

◆ **Tip:** Make a free exchange if you can.

◆ **Key elements:**

- Empathize with the customer's time, trouble, and good intent.
- Demonstrate cooperation.
- Inform the customer of possible costs.
- End with a "permission to proceed" question.

42. Your Equipment Is Unfairly Compared With Similar Products

◆ **Situation:** Your customer has had experience with equipment similar to yours and is quick to promote the differences. "The other one I looked at has a lot more features than yours does."

◆ **What you say:** "You may be right. I'm perhaps not as familiar with [that product] as you are. If you'd give me a list of the features that are important to you, I can find out if ours will do the same thing."

◆ **Why this works:** You will learn what's important to your customer's success. Shift from the features (which surely will not match) of the competing products to the more outstanding benefits yours provides.

◆ **Tip:** If your product does not have a feature your customer determines to be critical, suggest a substitute, an aftermarket device, a retro-fit, or a customization.

◆ **Key elements:**

- Accept the customer statement at face value.
- Ask for the corroborative details.
- Reinforce your product's superior merits.

SWIM

Sometimes it's hard to distinguish your business from the competitor's. All profess to care about the customer, promise great service, and swear to do everything they can for him. So how can you set yours apart from the others? Here's what one customer says about his automobile dealer.

"I don't think I've ever had such superior service from an auto dealer before. A limo from there to work and back, car washed and tank filled whenever I take the car in for regular service— I can't believe it! And they even call me later to see if I've got any new ideas for them or any complaints. Who could complain when you get treated so great!"

The service pleases him so much that he comes very close to stopping strangers on the street to suggest they buy cars from this company.

When you face a strong competitor, your best return will come from the pleased customer who speaks of you to others. Listen to your customers; think how others could make your own busy life easier. What can you do yourself or recommend to your boss that will cause your best customers to preach for you?

43. You Are Blamed For Bad Purchase

◆ **Situation:** Your customer asks for a particular product or part. She buys it, then finds it won't work for her problem. She brings the purchase back and tries to put the blame on you for the poor choice.

◆ **What you say:** "Ms. Customer, I know you put a lot of effort into this. As I see it, there are two things we can do now: reconstruct the paperwork to see who did what or we can figure out what we need to do to get your equipment up and running. Which would be the best use of your time?"

◆ **Why this works:** This helps the customer shift from finding fault to the more productive process of fixing the problem.

◆ **Tip:** Avoid turning a customer accusation into a win-lose event.

◆ **Key elements:**

- Acknowledge customer's investment of time.
- Give the customer options for the next step, including searching for blame.

44. Fulfillment Of An Outdated Request Is Demanded

◆ **Situation:** A guest comes in on a day of 100% hotel occupancy. She assures you she has a reservation for today, although she cannot find her confirmation slip. After some research, you realize her reservation was for yesterday, but now she is mad and demands a room immediately.

◆ **What you say:** "Gosh, what a shame about the mix-up! I've been there myself. And you're probably looking forward to a good night's sleep about now, too. Let me see what we can come up with here. If not here, I'll find you a room somewhere close. I'll call the bellman who can show you to the lounge for a drink or coffee—on us, of course—while we're seeing what we can find."

◆ **Why this works:** The customer is helpless, feeling out of control and perhaps afraid of being stranded. A take-charge attitude without patronizing the customer will help reduce the anxiety.

◆ **Tip:** When a customer is on-site and confrontive, and the solution will take you some time, find something to occupy her until you can get back to her with an answer.

◆ **Key elements:**

- Acknowledge your customer's frustration as well as your own.
- Take charge of the problem.
- Steer the customer away from a high traffic area.

45. Customer Refuses To Deal With Correct Person

◆ **Situation:** The complainant has been put off by another employee and refuses to go back to that worker, even though that person is the one with the answers.

◆ **What you say:** "I'm sorry your experience with _____ was unsatisfactory. I wish there was someone else with his expertise around here but he's really the best in the field. What are your ideas on how we might handle this?"

◆ **Why this works:** Without the customer's full awareness of the particulars and his cooperation, there is little you can do. If you can act on his idea, the outcome is more likely to succeed.

◆ **Tip:** When there are personality conflicts between a customer and a co-worker, avoid letting your own loyalty to one or the other affect your judgment.

◆ **Key elements:**

- Apologize.
- Explain your limitations.
- Ask for guidance from the customer.

46. Your Company Is Accused Of Dangerous Acts

◆ **Situation:** Your customer says, "Your electric company is evil; it's putting all of my family in danger!"

◆ **What you say:** "Specifically, what makes you certain you and your family have been put in danger?"

◆ **Why this works:** Until you know the particulars, you will be unable to figure out if the accusation is true (a low-level shock that indicates lack of grounding safeguards, for example) or off-base (evil extraterrestrials escaping from the wall socket).

◆ **Tip:** No matter how bizarre the statement, look for a rational basis first.

◆ **Key elements:**

- Ask for explicit details.
- Match the customer's words as closely as you can in fielding the question.

47. Conversation Begins With Anger

◆ **Situation:** When you answer the phone, your customer without warning begins speaking in a very angry and hostile manner. You don't know why.

◆ **What you say:** "Mr. Customer, I'm having a little trouble keeping up with you. Could you speak a little more slowly so I can be sure I don't miss anything?"

◆ **Why this works:** If you can assume the inadequacy for understanding the customer, you can often turn the customer into a helper. People who are angry frequently speak rapidly; a request to speak more slowly is less likely to cause the situation to escalate than if you tell the customer to calm down (a taboo in any case!).

◆ **Tip:** Request the least provocative action you can find that may lead to defusing.

◆ **Key elements:**

- Retain the responsibility for understanding.
- Request a specific, nonjudgmental action.
- Give the rationale for your request.

SINK

It's hard to understand why a company would prevent its employees from helping customers when no expense is involved. The cost of one lost transaction may be small, but what are the other costs when you implant that notion as an employee practice?

I live in a state where the old-fashioned service station still exists: an attendant fills the car gas tank. Our state has yet to okay the impersonal "If you want it, do it yourself" self-service gas station. As a result, I have not learned the various intricacies of gas pumps. On a recent business trip, I was running late and the tank was running low. I spent a moment at the pump trying to make sense out of the directions. Finally giving up, I sought out the attendants, two young men, about 18 years old, who sat behind the pay counter.

"Could you help me?" I asked, explaining my predicament. "Sure thing," answered one, as he jumped up from his chair and headed toward the door. "Wait a minute," cautioned his buddy, as he grabbed the other young man's arm, "We can't do that." Then he turned to me. "Look, lady, he's new around here and doesn't know better. Even though we'd like to show you how to use the pump, we'd get fired if our boss ever caught us. Can't tell you where to get help either."

Bosses who prevent employees from going the next step for customers will surely never have employees who will go the next step for the boss.

---

48. Anger At Earlier Treatment Is Expressed

◆ **Situation:** While you were out, your co-worker mishandled a customer and really made him mad. How do you smooth it over without making your co-worker look stupid (even though she might be)?

◆ **What you say:** "Mr. Customer, you should not have to put up with anything but the best from us. Please let me make it right for you by giving top priority to your situation."

◆ **Why this works:** When you tell the customer how he should have been treated and how you intend to make amends, you can draw attention away from your co-worker's behavior.

◆ **Tip:** Focus on what should have happened rather than on what actually happened.

◆ **Key elements:**

  • Express your dissatisfaction with the way the matter was handled.
  • Describe what should have occurred.
  • Offer your best recommendation.

49. Customer Refuses To Let You Explain

◆ **Situation:** Your customer explodes with anger, rebuking you and your company at great length. You try interrupting but have no success.

◆ **What you say:** When you discover a nonstop talker, don't say anything at all: no "unh-hunh," no "I see," nothing. Eventually the customer will ask, "Are you still there?" And then you say: "Yes, sir, and I've been keeping careful notes. Is there anything else to add?"

◆ **Why this works:** Customers need feedback sooner or later. When they are ready, you can take charge with a carefully crafted phrase. Take seriously their remarks and encourage full disclosure.

◆ **Tip:** Place your forefinger lightly across your mouth as a reminder to keep silent.

◆ **Key elements:**

- Keep absolutely silent until you are invited to speak.
- Take notes and tell the customer you have been doing so.
- Ask for more information.

SWIM

Do you remember when you were a small child and you moved from one house to another? Lots of anxiety surrounded that move and many questions. For example, "How will Grandma know where to find me?" When a business moves from one location to another, a similar anxiety surfaces: "How will they ever find us?" Here's one delivery man that had no trouble, it seems.

"That UPS guy we've got—would you believe he tracked me down to deliver that package! How do you suppose he figured out where we moved to? I don't think I even had chance to tell anyone about our new address. I'd hate to be a crook on the run and have this guy on my tail!"

There are those customer service professionals who see themselves as detectives, looking for the clues and searching for the evidence that will result in the answer to a customer's problem. Are you the one who delights in discovery or the one who is annoyed by the nuisance?

50. Customer Refuses To Explain His Concern

◆ **Situation:** Your caller is very angry, but for some reason he won't explain the problem. He hangs up, then calls back immediately. He won't give his name or any other information. He is just angry and wants something done.

◆ **What you say:** "Mr. Customer, it's very clear something really disturbing has happened. Please let me get to the bottom of it. If you had an idea about what I could do, what would it be?"

◆ **Why this works:** Events can get so out of hand that all a customer can do is sputter angrily. If you can help him focus on the end result, as if the problem were defined, you can often break the log jam.

◆ **Key elements:**

  • Acknowledge the customer's despair.
  • Speak convincingly and with fervor of your genuine desire to assist.
  • Begin with the end.

51. Customer Refuses To Listen To Reason

◆ **Situation:** Your customer is so angry she hears nothing you say. Her only interest seems to be in staying angry with your company.

◆ **What you say:** "It's perfectly understandable why you feel the way you do. And it sounds like there's nothing I can do to change your impression of our company. Is that right?"

◆ **Why this works:** When your best judgment is that you've done everything you can and your customer is still unreachable, tell the customer of your conclusion. This will let you end the matter. The next step is up to your customer.

◆ **Tip:** You will not be able to resolve every complaint brought to you by a customer. Expect some personal disappointment occasionally.

◆ **Key elements:**

  • Accept your customer's view that the complaint cannot be resolved.
  • Get their agreement to your assessment of their position on the matter.

52. In Spite Of Evidence To The Contrary, Customer Insists On Being Right

◆ **Situation:** It seems like your customer's goals are to be right, quarrel, stay mad, and not listen to everything you say.

◆ **What you say:** "There's no way I can argue with anything you've said other than to go back over it all again. That would probably be a waste of both your time and mine. If we assume both of us are right in our perceptions, I'd like to suggest an alternative we can both live with."

Variation: "There's no way I can argue with anything you've said other than to go back over it all again. That would probably be a waste of both your time and mine. Since you seem so definite about this matter and reluctant to discuss any options that we can both live with, I don't see anything I can do other than to proceed with what I understand to be the original agreement which means..."

◆ **Why this works:** Offering a third alternative furnishes your customer with a face-saving out. If that is refused and you need to act, the original agreement is the safest choice.

◆ **Tip:** Keep your supervisor informed.

◆ **Key elements:**

- Avoid arguing with a customer.
- Suggest a third alternative.
- Return to the original agreement if the impasse persists.

53. You Are Accused Of Having A Bad Attitude

◆ **Situation:** Even though you have worked very hard, and you think professionally, to resolve your customer's complaint, she accuses you of a variety of hostile attitudes: "You're not being very nice," "You're getting nasty," or "You're really testy today, aren't you?"

◆ **What you say:** "I'm disappointed that you have that impression of me. How might I change your perception?"

◆ **Why this works:** Demonstrating a sincere interest in learning what has upset your customer can give you the information you need to turn your customer's attitude around.

◆ **Tip:** This is an excellent time to learn, if you don't get tripped up by your own defensiveness. Your customer could be right!

◆ **Key elements:**

- Express your perplexity.
- Ask for clarification.

SINK

Although it's not a law anywhere, consider making an adjustment when your mistakes inconvenience your customer. Sometimes a simple apology will do; sometimes the error calls for another strategy.

The two couples had just finished dinner in the resort's most expensive restaurant and were recounting their adventure.

"Let's see: Dinner cost the four of us $20 a piece plus wine; that's about $100. She didn't get here with the salad for 45 minutes. And then the waiter told us 10 minutes after we ordered that they had run out of the entree we wanted and we had to start all over. We had to send stuff back because it was cold. And don't forget, the fondue sterno caught the table on fire! And would you believe, three and a half hours later, all the manager could say was this should never have happened and then he laughed!? What do you think—should we leave a tip?"

It's okay to laugh at your mistakes; humor is good. However, as the incident may not be funny for your customer, temper it with thoughtfulness and consideration for the inconvenience caused your customer.

54. Uninterrupted Foul Language Is Used

◆ **Situation:** Your customer uses foul language repeatedly and won't stop.

◆ **What you say:** Don't interrupt. Hold the phone away from your ear if necessary, because there is little you can do about folks who act in this unprofessional way. Don't say anything at all until they run down, and eventually they will. And then you say: "Mr. Customer, I understand how strongly you feel about this matter and I've made very careful notes of everything you've told me, which I plan to discuss with my boss. Is there anything else you would like him to know?"

◆ **Why this works:** When you highlight the action you plan to take and then ask a straightforward, unemotional question, you will help your customer get back in control. Knowing that you are taking notes and mentioning your boss in a nonthreatening manner helps as well.

◆ **Tip:** The physical act of writing will help you avoid getting baited by the customer.

◆ **Key elements:**

  • Ignore bad language.
  • Sort out and write down the facts.
  • Take the same steps you would take with a customer who uses more acceptable words.
  • Ask for additional information.

55. You Are Accused Of Lack Of Interest

◆ **Situation:** You don't have the information to help your customer. He believes otherwise. He says, "It's obvious you don't care about me or my business or you'd fix this."

◆ **What you say:** "Mr. Customer, given the lack of attention to this matter, I can see why you believe we don't care. I'm at the end of my rope as to exactly what I can do to fix it. But I promise you I won't let it drop. As soon as I hang up, I'll get an appointment with the department manager and then I'll call you. I expect I can get back to you this afternoon between 3 and 4 if that's okay."

◆ **Why this works:** Because we want to please our customers, when we can't it seems easier to ignore the problem instead of acknowledging it. By validating the customer's point of view and sharing your own frustration, you can repair the relationship and search for an appropriate resolution.

◆ **Tip:** When you absolutely can do nothing, your first priority is to shore up the relationship so the customer will still want to do business with you.

◆ **Key elements:**

- Restate your customer's position.
- Express your own disappointment with the failure.
- Tell him specifically how you plan to address the problem.

SWIM

In spite of your best intentions, mistakes occur and you inconvenience your customer.

It was one of those cold, blustery, Pacific Northwest wintery days when I purchased a fax machine. When I got to the office and began to put it together, I discovered that a critical cord was missing. With some frustration and no hope of getting any help from the store, I called the store manager.

"I'm real sorry the cord for the fax machine you just bought here didn't get included in the package. It's a long way for you to drive back here—must take about 30 minutes one way I guess. Tell you what—even though our delivery to your part of town isn't till tomorrow, we'll get a courier to bring it to you this afternoon. I want you to start using that machine right away. I also want you to know that doing business with our business discount store is better than doing business with any other in town."

If your company has many options available to help a customer when plans go askew, your company will be the one customers will return to.

56. Customer Complains Loudly And Publicly

◆ **Situation:** Your customer complains so loudly that other people in the area can overhear.

◆ **What you say:** "Mr. Customer, I probably can get this matter straightened out fairly quickly if we can get away from all these other distractions. Let's step over here where it's a little more private and then I can give my full attention to just exactly what occurred."

◆ **Why this works:** This demonstrates your interest in solving the problem, your intent to concentrate on this issue alone, and your willingness to hear him out.

◆ **Tip:** You may not have a restricted area readily available, so look around now and select a secluded spot to have a private conversation with a distraught customer. When a customer is visibly upset, for your own concentration you need to eliminate all possible distractions. Remain at arm's length. If you must touch the customer, use no more than a light touch at the elbow.

◆ **Key elements:**

  • Describe your need for privacy.
  • Emphasize your intent to address the matter.

57. Customer Lies Deliberately

◆ **Situation:** You know your customer is telling an outright lie.

◆ **What you say:** "Mr. Customer, there must have been a misunderstanding of some sort. We have always had a one-year warranty, not 18 months. Would you like me to rewrap it for you or have the service department take a look at it and give you an estimate of the costs for repair?"

◆ **Why this works:** When you manage the matter as a misunderstanding, you give your customer a way out of a graceless situation. If you immediately suggest several actions (including a "do-nothing" action), you may be able to avoid a futile argument about conditions you can't change.

◆ **Tip:** Avoid confronting lies or other discrepancies if your only purpose is to prove the customer is a liar. You know he is and he knows he is; get on with the business at hand.

◆ **Key elements:**

- Address the matter as a misunderstanding.
- State the facts as you know them to be.
- Give the customer two options: do nothing or fix it at his expense.

58. Suspicion Is Aroused When Seeking Redress

◆ **Situation:** Your customer:
May be a thief or shoplifter trying to get cash.
May have found the merchandise.
May be trying to "cheat" on the warranty.
May be angling for an undeserved punitive settlement.
May not actually own the merchandise.
May have abused the merchandise.
May have deliberately violated the warranty.

◆ **What you say:** "Mr. Customer, I wish I could do what you're asking because we would like to keep you as a customer. Unfortunately, the way this type of transaction is handled is pretty well cast in stone and only the general manager can approve any adjustment of that sort. Shall I set up an appointment?"

◆ **Why this works:** When you doubt the reliability of your customer, this approach will give you the opportunity to check out your misgivings with another without alienating a customer who is legitimate.

◆ **Tip:** Avoid arguing or accusing.

◆ **Key elements:**

- Express your interest in cooperating.
- Describe the approval process.
- Ask the customer's approval to proceed.

59. Customer Believes You're Making Excuses For Your Poor Service

◆ **Situation:** You are always at fault with this customer. And most of the time the errors happen because of uncontrollable elements such as weather delays. You call him as soon as you know there's going to be a problem, but it's happened so many times now that he thinks you're just making excuses.

◆ **What you say:** "Mr. Customer, I don't know what to say except again to apologize for the delay. It seems like no matter how hard we try, your orders seem to fall into a black hole. But I for one am going to make this my personal responsibility to see to it that it doesn't happen again. Here's what I plan to do to get things back on track now and in the future."

◆ **Why this works:** When you acknowledge what the customer already knows rather than pretend the events never occurred, you defuse a potentially embarrassing scene. The "fail-safe" promise tells the customer you are earnest about ensuring a problem-free future with your company.

◆ **Tip:** If you intend to keep this customer, red-flag the account so everyone will know the significance of future transactions.

◆ **Key elements:**

- Apologize for the problems.
- Make this customer your personal responsibility and tell him so.
- Tell the customer how the problem will be fixed.

SINK

To a customer, the cost of research for an equipment purchase and the dependence on you to follow through is no small matter.

"Here is my order for the computer, the printer, and the software just as we worked out. And you say you'll have it here in two weeks? Great!" Four weeks later: "When do you expect my computer order to be in? Another two weeks? Well, okay." Ten weeks later: "What do you mean, you've lost my order and we have to start over? Couldn't you have called me? Doesn't anyone follow up on these things?"

It should be no surprise that performance bonds are now a common practice in contracts because many vendors have failed to come through as agreed.

60. Preferential Treatment Is Requested

◆ **Situation:** Your customer wants his order processed now even though others came in before his.

◆ **What you say:** "Here's how I may be able to help you out without being unfair to our other clients who called in earlier."

◆ **Why this works:** This tells your customer you want to do what is asked, yet also explains why you may have to take other circumstances into consideration.

◆ **Tip:** Use this statement if it's important to make the customer aware of a "waiting line." You may know the customer is asking for special treatment; the customer may not know. Otherwise handle the transaction as you would any other request.

◆ **Key elements:**

- Establish your interest in meeting your customer's needs.
- Clarify your rationale for suggesting a solution other than the preferred.

61. Your Costs Are Unfavorably Compared To Those Of A Competitor

◆ **Situation:** Your customer says she can get the same thing down the street and at a lower price.

◆ **What you say:** "Ms. Customer, you could very well be right about that. But many years ago, our company decided their goals were to provide flawless service and the highest quality they could, rather than be the cheapest vendor in town. That's why I work here, too, and why we have so many long-term satisfied customers."

◆ **Why this works:** Customers need to justify for themselves or for others that they are getting their money's worth, whatever the price. A brief explanation with backup documentation will usually suffice.

◆ **Tip:** If you find yourself apologetic about your prices, you may be subconsciously influencing your customer's perception. Take time out to examine your own beliefs.

◆ **Key elements:**

- Acknowledge the validity of your customer's perception.
- Reinforce the benefits your product provides.
- Support the company mission.
- Offer third party evidence.

SWIM

One way to endear yourself to customers and reduce complaints about service charges is to teach them how to do the simple things themselves. It means knowing your product inside and out, understanding how the customer (an amateur most likely) may see the same piece of equipment, and using nontechnical language.

"You don't have a service contract on your copy machine and I sure hate to come out if it's working okay. It'll cost you $85 and that's a lot of money if you don't need anything done. The only thing I'd do besides clean it up real good is check those orange 'fingers' on the roller to be sure that carbon doesn't build up. If there is any, just scrape it off with your fingernail. Be sure you do it when it's cold so you don't get burned. That should take care of it."

Educating your customer rather than exploiting their ignorance is always good policy.

62. You Are Asked To Do Unauthorized Work

◆ **Situation:** You have made a service call to fix a customer's equipment. While you are there, another employee asks you to "tell me what's wrong with this darn thing. It'll only take a minute." You want to avoid creating an unhappy customer.

◆ **What you say:** "I'd be happy to take a look at the _____. I'll get the okay from my office and in the meantime you can get this work order signed. Should I go ahead and make the call? Do you have a phone handy?"

◆ **Why this works:** You confirm you want to help by detailing the procedure, thus avoiding either one of you getting into trouble.

◆ **Tip:** Be wary of "it'll only take a minute" requests that your company may have to bill for and that your customer may not have authorized.

◆ **Key elements:**

- Restate the customer's request.
- Explain your procedure.
- Get agreement to the conditions before proceeding.

63. You Are Put On The Defensive

◆ **Situation:** Your customer asks, "Why do you people charge so much?" *or* "Why doesn't anyone there ever return my calls?"

◆ **What you say:** "Could you give me a little more background about...what you heard about our charges?...*or*...about what happened with your phone calls?"

◆ **Why this works:** When you request more information, you will be able to find out what's really troubling the customer. It can also help reduce your tendency to overreact.

◆ **Tip:** "Why" questions usually are not really questions, but accusations, and that's what leads to defensiveness. But nobody can put you the defensive. This is the position you choose based on your own internal self-talk.

◆ **Key elements:**

- Check your emotions.
- Ask for specific information.

Practice: Stimulus Statements

Here is a chance to try out the scripts on the preceding pages. Read the stimulus statement (that's what a customer uses to stimulate you to act!) and draft your own version in the space provided. Then review the "What you say" portion of the scripts on pages 51-110 and note the reference scripts you think also would apply.

Customer: "I'm John Smith. They told me my plans would be here last week. But they weren't. I want to know what's going on down there."

Your response:

Why do you think this will work:

Reference Script #:

Customer: "I've been a real good customer here for a long time, and now you're telling me you still can't give me a break? How can you do this to me?"

Your response:

Why do you think this will work:

Reference Script #:

Customer: "Are you calling me a liar? Why, you incompetent bunch of_____! All that rain must have rusted your brains! Let me talk to your supervisor where I can get some straight answers."

Your response:

Why do you think this will work:

Reference Script #:

Customer: "What do you mean you can't do that? That's not what they told me! Don't they tell all you guys the same thing?"

Your response:

Why do you think this will work:

Reference Script #:

Chapter Seven

At-A-Glance Summary

Survival Strategies
- Use a complaint management system
- Use a systematic complaint management process
- Listen to learn
- Understand escalation
- Take care of yourself

Complaint Management System
- The goal
- Guiding principles
- A systematic problem-solving process
- The method

Exposure Protection
- Knowledge
- Act-as-if principal
- Keeping track of customers

Knowledge
- Your company
- Your products and services
- Customers
- Salesmanship

- Functional knowledge
- Technical knowledge
- Business economy

Rules For Exposure Reduction
- Perception is the truth
- Fix the problem, don't fix blame
- Don't take it personally
- Empathize, don't sympathize
- Don't confess your sins
- Educate for future perfect, don't condemn for failing at past perfect
- Eliminate the word "why" from your vocabulary
- Apply the platinum rule
- Avoid defensiveness
- The customer is all you have; every decision you make must be based on this awareness

Exposure Avoidance—The Tools
- Customer surveys
- Employee surveys
- Focus groups
- Employee/customer problem-solving groups
- Training
- Complaint logs
- Ongoing complaint analysis
- Brainstorming for zero-defect standard
- Complaint case studies for universal examination
- Benchmarking

Exposure Recovery
- Recovery process
- Sentence maps
- Open-ended questions
- Clarifying responses
- Empathic response
- Special situation

Recovery Process
- Devote your complete attention to the customer
- Take all the time necessary
- Eliminate all distractions and interruptions
- Take notes
- Use the Complaint Management Model
- Familiarize yourself with Sentence Maps
- Use the Exposure Recovery Scripts

Exposure Recovery Scripts—Summary

1. **ALL THE PHONES RING AT ONCE**
   - Smile, give your company's name.
   - Decide how much control to allow the caller.

2. **ON-HOLD IS A CHRONIC CONDITION**
   - Know your system's shortcomings.
   - Acknowledge the customer's feeling state.
   - Take charge.
   - Begin problem-solving immediately.

3. **YOU'RE FACE-TO-FACE AND THE PHONE RINGS**
   - First come, first served.
   - Ask permission of your walk-in customer.
   - Make a call-back appointment with your phone caller.

4. **CO-WORKER DOES NOT RETURN PHONE CALLS**
   - Empathize with the customer's inconvenience.
   - Provide alternatives.
   - Specify by name and rank the individual who will be talking with the customer in place of your co-worker.

5. **TAKING A MESSAGE FOR A NONRESPONSIVE CO-WORKER**
   - Acknowledge the customer's request.
   - Promise only what you can deliver.

6. **FOLLOW-THROUGH FAILS**
   - Empathize with the customer.
   - Clarify the information.
   - Take action.

7. **BACKLOG HAMPERS HANDLING**
   - Explain the personnel change.
   - Clarify the information needed.
   - Assure the customer that you personally are on top of the situation and will take action.

8. **INFORMATION UNAVAILABLE WHEN PROMISED**
   - Acknowledge the difficulty.
   - Make a personal commitment.
   - Allow for a possible continued delay.

9. **SUPERVISOR INTERVENTION IS REQUESTED**
   - Acknowledge the legitimacy of the customer's request.
   - Escalate to a level where the problem can be resolved.
   - Keep control of the request.

10. **CARELESS CO-WORKER MISHANDLES CUSTOMER TRANSACTION**
    - Acknowledge the customer's concern.
    - Set the performance standard.
    - Provide your customer with an alternative for future reference.

11. **DELAY OCCURS—ANOTHER DEPARTMENT**
    - Inform the customer immediately of the delay.
    - Confirm your next action.
    - Ask the customer's opinion.

12. **DELAY OCCURS—YOUR VENDOR**
    - Acknowledge the problem.
    - Confirm your next action.
    - Ask the customer's opinion.

13. **DELAY OCCURS—CUSTOMER'S VENDOR**
    - Clarify without blaming.
    - Refer the customer to his vendor.
    - Provide a life line for follow-up.

14. **EQUIPMENT IS UNRELIABLE**
    - Empathize with the customer.
    - State your company's equal concern.
    - Present a plan of action.
    - Ask for the customer's thoughts.

15. **ERROR RESULTS IN OVERCHARGE**
    - Empathize with the customer.
    - Express your similiar feeling.
    - Correct the error.

16. **CHRONIC PRODUCT FAILURE OCCURS**
    - Thank your customer.
    - Act on it immediately.
    - Connect your expert with your customer.
    - Determine timing.
    - Provide the opportunity for technician-to-technician talk.

17. **CONTROL IS OUT OF YOUR HANDS**
    - Empathize with your customer.
    - Share your like frustration.
    - Prepare a plan to activate upon immediate elimination of the obstacle.
    - Get the customer's agreement.

18. **EXPECTATIONS ARE NOT MET—*PRODUCT***
    - Acknowledge the discrepancy without placing blame.
    - Present options with cost range.

19. **EXPECTATIONS ARE NOT MET—*DISTRIBUTOR SERVICE***
    - Acknowledge your customer's experience.
    - State the uniqueness of the request.
    - Investigate.
    - Gain the customer's agreement.

20. **EXPECTATIONS ARE NOT MET—*REPAIR TIME***
    - Acknowledge the inconvenience.
    - Explain briefly the technical nature of the problem.
    - Flag for priority treatment.
    - Confirm the mutual desire for a quality solution.

21. **EXPECTATIONS ARE NOT MET—*TIME FRAME***
    - Educate your customer.
    - Reinforce the integrity of your organization.
    - Avoid blaming customers for their shortsightedness.
    - Offer options.
    - Let the customer decide.

22. **SOLUTION REQUESTED IS ILLEGAL**
    - Explain briefly the law. (Do not make excuses.)
    - Outline briefly the penalties. (Do not dwell on them.)
    - Empathize with the customer's position.
    - Refer him to someone who can hear his concerns and possibly make a difference.
    - Ask permission to refer.

23. **SOLUTION REQUESTED IS TOO COSTLY**
    - Research all possibilities.
    - Explain briefly your limitations.
    - Refer to your supervisor.

24. **CUSTOMER DEMANDS CO-WORKER FIRING**
    - Thank the customer.
    - Reassure him that action will be taken.
    - Safeguard confidentiality.
    - Focus on protecting his account

25. **SELF-RELIANCE FAILS TO CORRECT A PROBLEM**
    - Acknowledge the customer's work and frustration level.
    - Underline the need for quality attention for effective resolution.
    - Give a realistic time frame or set of conditions.
    - Bring technical experts together or with the user.

26. **INTEGRITY OF BUSINESS IS QUESTIONED**
    - Paraphrase his words.
    - Offer information to counter his belief.

27. **RESPONSIBILITY IS DENIED BY CUSTOMER**
    - Acknowledge your customer's experience and frustration.
    - Fix the problem.
    - Identify a reference for future use.

28. **INVOICE WAS NOT SUBMITTED**
    - Acknowledge your customer's anxiety.
    - State in positive terms the action the customer needs to take and the action you will take.
    - Give a time frame the customer can count on.

29. **PAPERWORK IS INCOMPLETE—*INSTRUCTIONS NOT FOLLOWED***
    - Acknowledge the customer's point of view.
    - Assist him immediately.
    - Fix the problem; don't fix blame.

30. **SERVICE CHARGE IS "TOO HIGH"**
    - Use the words that allow both you and the customer to save face.
    - Offer a review of each piece of the transaciton to clarify the major sensitive area.
    - Adjust charges if allowable.

31. **NOTHING SATISFIES THE CUSTOMER**
    - Empathize.
    - Become a partner with your customer by showing a concern equal to hers.

• Ask for her ideas.

32. PRODUCT IS UNAVAILABLE
• Acknowledge the customer's interest in your product.
• Explain briefly your limitations.
• Give her an option she can pursue.

33. PERSONALITIES CONFLICT
• Label the roadblock for both you and the customer.
• Ask for your customer's help.

34. YOU HAVE NO AUTHORITY TO ACT
• Accept the request at face value.
• Escalate to the next highest level—keeping the customer with you.
• Explain the situation to your supervisor.
• Acknowledge courteously your customer's contribution.

35. YOU ARE ACCUSED OF BEING RUDE
• Acknowledge her feeling.
• Apologize for the customer's perception.
• Ask for information.

36. CUSTOMER RESISTS CHANGES IN HOW YOU APPLY THE COMPANY POLICY
• Acknowledge the customer's valid distress and confusion.
• Reinforce the customer's value to the company.
• Create a transition plan.
• Gain acceptance.

37. EXCEPTIONAL PAYMENT TREATMENT IS REQUESTED
• Create a link between the stressful issue and a solution.
• Show your commitment.
• Emphasize your mutual interests.
• Suggest a remedy.

38. EXCEPTIONAL CREDIT PREFERENCE IS REQUESTED
• Restate the agreement.
• Describe the boundaries or limitations.
• Inform the customer about possible resources.

39. DELIVERY PREFERENCE IS REQUESTED
• Summarize your customer's position and your business practice.

- Present a plan you can live with.
- Arrange for a special time to iron out the details.
- Press for a specific next step.

40. MANUAL INSTRUCTIONS ARE QUESTIONED
- Recognize your customer's frustration.
- Get the particulars of the pivotal problem.
- Use your customer's efforts as your building base.

41. PROBLEM IS MISDIAGNOSED BECAUSE OF OVERCONFIDENCE
- Empathize with the customer's time, trouble, and good intent.
- Demonstrate cooperation.
- Inform the customer of possible costs.
- End with a permission to proceed question.

42. YOUR EQUIPMENT IS UNFAIRLY COMPARED WITH SIMILAR PRODUCTS
- Accept the customer statement at face value.
- Ask for the corroborative details.
- Reinforce your product's superior merits.

43. YOU ARE BLAMED FOR BAD PURCHASE
- Acknowledge customer's investment of time.
- Give the customer options for the next step, including searching for blame.

44. FULFILLMENT OF AN OUTDATED REQUEST IS DEMANDED
- Acknowledge your customer's frustration as well as your own.
- Take charge of the problem.
- Steer the customer away from a high traffic area.

45. CUSTOMER REFUSES TO DEAL WITH CORRECT PERSON
- Apologize.
- Explain your limitations.
- Ask for guidance from the customer.

46. YOUR COMPANY IS ACCUSED OF DANGEROUS ACTS
- Ask for explicit details.
- Match the customer's words as closely as you can in fielding the question.

47. CONVERSATION BEGINS WITH ANGER
- Retain the responsibility for understanding.
- Request a specific nonjudgmental action.
- Give the rationale for your request.

48. ANGER AT EARLIER TREATMENT IS EXPRESSED
- Express your dissatisfaction with the way the matter was handled.
- Describe what should have occurred.
- Offer your best recommendation.

49. CUSTOMER REFUSES TO LET YOU EXPLAIN
- Keep absolutely silent until you are invited to speak.
- Take notes and tell the customer you have been doing so.
- Ask for more information.

50. CUSTOMER REFUSES TO EXPLAIN HIS CONCERN
- Acknowledge the customer's despair.
- Speak convincingly and with fervor of your genuine desire to assist.
- Begin with the end.

51. CUSTOMER REFUSES TO LISTEN TO REASON
- Accept your customer's view that the complaint cannot be resolved.
- Get their agreement to your assessment of their position on the matter.

52. IN SPITE OF EVIDENCE TO THE CONTRARY, CUSTOMER INSISTS ON BEING RIGHT
- Avoid arguing with a customer.
- Suggest a third alternative.
- Return to the original agreement if the impasse persists.

53. YOU ARE ACCUSED OF HAVING A BAD ATTITUDE
- Express your perplexity.
- Ask for clarification.

54. UNINTERRUPTED FOUL LANGUAGE IS USED
- Ignore bad language.
- Sort out and write down the facts.
- Take the same steps you would take with a customer who uses more acceptable words.
- Ask for additional information.

55. YOU ARE ACCUSED OF LACK OF INTEREST
- Restate your customer's position.

- Express your own disappointment with the failure.
- Tell him specifically how you plan to address the problem.

56. CUSTOMER COMPLAINS LOUDLY AND PUBLICLY
- Describe your need for privacy.
- Emphasize your intent to address the matter.

57. CUSTOMER LIES DELIBERATELY
- Address the matter as a misunderstanding.
- State the facts as you know them to be.
- Give the customer two options: do nothing or fix it at his expense.

58. SUSPICION IS AROUSED WHEN SEEKING REDRESS
- Express your interest in cooperating.
- Describe the approval process.
- Ask the customer's approval to proceed.

59. CUSTOMER BELIEVES YOU'RE MAKING EXCUSES FOR YOUR POOR SERVICE
- Apologize for the problems.
- Make this customer your personal responsibility and tell him so.
- Tell the customer how the problem will be fixed.

60. PREFERENTIAL TREATMENT IS REQUESTED
- Establish your interest in meeting your customer's needs.
- Clarify your rationale for suggesting a solution other than the preferred.

61. YOUR COSTS ARE UNFAVORABLY COMPARED TO THOSE OF A COMPETITOR
- Acknowledge the validity of your customer's perception.
- Reinforce the benefits your product provides.
- Support the company mission.
- Offer third party evidence.

62. YOU ARE ASKED TO DO UNAUTHORIZED WORK
- Restate the customer's request
- Explain your procedure.
- Get agreement to the conditions before proceeding.

63. YOU ARE PUT ON THE DEFENSIVE
- Check your emotions.
- Ask for specific information.

Conclusion

The use of these applications is based on my own experience. I know they work. They work in my business and for my clients. It's up to you to apply them and adapt them specifically to work for you. When they don't work, put them on the shelf for future use or throw them out. And then tell me about your experience. I will be happy to respond promptly to any written request from you to overcome obstacles facing your operations.

Bernice B. Johnston, CPC, President
Milestone Unlimited, Inc.
0225 SW Montgomery St., #4
Portland, OR 97201

Or you can FAX me: Or you can phone me:
(503) 224-9534   (503) 224-8610

I'd like to hear from you!

Through Milestone Unlimited, Inc., you can receive training, consultation (on-site and by phone), workbooks, audio tapes, and monographs in the following areas:

- AIDS awareness
- board of director advancement
- business and strategic planning
- business alliance programs
- communication improvement systems
- community relations
- conflict management
- customer service applications
- drug-testing policies and procedures
- employee surveys
- employee involvement systems
- executive development
- goal setting
- handling customer complaints
- internal customer service
- interpersonal communication skills
- leadership development
- listening
- management audits
- marketing
- meeting effectiveness
- organization development
- participative management
- pay-for-performance alternatives
- performance appraisal systems
- personal and professional career management planning
- public speaking
- sales effectiveness
- sexual harassment audits
- stress management
- supervisor and management development
- team development
- time management
- total quality management service strategies

Grow Your Business With
America's #1 Small Business Series

Mancuso's Small Business Resource Guide by Joseph R. Mancuso
The names, addresses, and numbers of the best sources of information for your business.
208 pages, ISBN 1-57071-066-X (paperback)

Your First Business Plan by Joseph Covello and Brian Hazelgren
Learn the critical steps to writing a winning business plan. Includes complete sample plan.
152 pages, ISBN 0-942061-47-0 (hardcover) • ISBN 1-57071-044-9 (paperback)

Great Idea! Now What? by Howard Bronson and Peter Lange
Turn your idea, invention, or business concept into a moneymaking success!
224 pages, ISBN 1-57071-039-2 (paperback)

The Internet Business Primer by Wayne Allison
A concise, nontechnical guide to identifying opportunities for your business on the Internet.
160 pages, ISBN 1-57071-064-3 (paperback)

The Small Business Legal Guide by Lynne Ann Frasier, Esq.
The complete legal reference for your vital business concerns. Includes forms you can use.
176 pages, ISBN 1-57071-060-0 (paperback)

Smart Hiring by Robert W. Wendover
Everything you need to know to find and hire the best employees.
200 pages, ISBN 0-942061-57-8 (hardcover) • ISBN 0-942061-56-X (paperback)

The Small Business Start-Up Guide by Hal Root and Steve Koenig
A surefire blueprint for launching your business. Includes individual state requirements.
152 pages, ISBN 0-942061-70-5 (hardcover) • ISBN 0-942061-67-5 (paperback)

Getting Paid In Full by W. Kelsea Wilber
Collect the money you are owed and develop system to train customers to pay on time.
144 pages, ISBN 0-942061-71-3 (hardcover) • ISBN 0-942061-68-3 (paperback)

Protect Your Business by Sgt. James Nelson and Ofc. Terry Davis
Step-by-step ways to safeguard your business against shoplifting, employee theft, and more.
144 pages, ISBN 0-942061-66-7 (paperback)

Mancuso's Small Business Basics by Joseph R. Mancuso
America's bestselling small business author shows you how to create a successful business.
188 pages, ISBN 1-57071-076-7 (paperback)

To order these books or any other of our many publications, *please contact your local bookseller* or call Sourcebooks at 708-961-3900. Get a copy of our catalog by writing or faxing:

Sourcebooks Inc.
P. O. Box 372
Naperville, IL 60566
(708) 961-3900
FAX: (708) 961-2168

WARNER MEMORIAL LIBRARY
EASTERN COLLEGE
ST. DAVIDS, PA. 19087